MAKING A COMPLAINT

Other How To Books for Family Reference

Applying for Legal Aid
Arranging Insurance
Buying a Personal Computer
Cash from Your Computer
Choosing a Nursing Home
Choosing a Package Holiday
Dealing with a Death in the Family
Helping Your Child to Read
How to Apply to an Industrial
   Tribunal
How to be a Local Councillor
How to be an Effective School
   Governor
How to Claim State Benefits
How to Lose Weight & Keep Fit

How to Plan a Wedding
How to Raise Funds & Sponsorship
How to Run a Local Campaign
How to Run a Voluntary Group
How to Survive Divorce
How To Take Care of Your Heart
How to Use the Internet
Making a Wedding Speech
Managing Your Personal Finances
Successful Grandparenting
Successful Single Parenting
Taking in Students
Teaching Someone to Drive
Winning Consumer Competitions

Other titles in preparation

The How To series now contains more than 170 titles in the following categories:

Business Basics
Family Reference
Jobs & Careers
Living & Working Abroad
Student Handbooks
Successful Writing

Please send for a free copy of the latest catalogue for full details (see back cover for address).

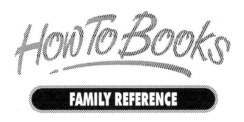

FAMILY REFERENCE

MAKING A COMPLAINT

How to put your case successfully
and win redress

Helen Shay

How To Books

By the same author in this series

Copyright & Law for Writers: How to protect yourself and your creative work

Cartoons by Mike Flanagan

British Library Cataloguing in Publication Data
A catalogue record for this book is available from the British Library.

First published in 1996 by How To Books Ltd, Plymbridge House, Estover Road, Plymouth PL6 7PZ, United Kingdom. Tel: (01752) 202301. Fax: (01752) 202331.

Note: The material contained in this book is set out in good faith for general guidance and no liability can be accepted for loss or expense incurred as a result of relying in particular circumstances on statements made in the book. The laws and regulations are complex and liable to change, and readers should check the current position with the relevant authorities before making personal arrangements.

Produced for How To Books by Deer Park Productions.
Typeset by PDQ Typesetting, Stoke-on-Trent, Staffs.
Printed and bound by Cromwell Press, Broughton Gifford, Melksham, Wiltshire.

Contents

List of Illustrations

Foreword

Consumers of today are frequently entering contracts for goods and services with increasing complexity. It is vitally important that they are knowledgeable in their rights, and that adequate mechanisms of redress are in place should things go wrong.

Often consumer disputes are settled in the small claims section of the County Court. It may be that many of these proceedings can be avoided, or alternative methods can be used.

Local authority departments and voluntary organisations increasingly offer a free advice service – not only making available information on consumer law, but also assistance in dispute resolution. It may be that providing a leaflet or relevant telephone number is all that is required, but often the advice service can work pro-actively for the consumer.

Much consumer legislation still upholds the maxim of *caveat emptor* (let the buyer beware). An understanding of the basic legal concepts can go a long way to alleviate any frustration and dissatisfaction.

As consumers become better informed, they are more selective with the goods and services which they purchase, thereby pushing up overall standards.

This book fulfils an important function in providing information to consumers and raising awareness of the issues as they affect us all.

Trevor Simpson
Trading Standards Officer

Acknowledgements

I would like to thank all those people and agencies, such as the Office of Fair Trading, Trading Standards Departments, the Data Protection Registry and the Lord Chancellor's Department, who have provided me with information in writing this book. Form N1 is Crown Copyright and reproduced with the kind permission of the Controller of Her Majesty's Stationery Office. Finally, I am grateful to the many colleagues and friends in different legal fields with whom I have had the privilege to work over the years.

Preface

'Justice delayed is justice denied'.

(Gladstone 1809–1898)

Anyone who has ever had a complaint knows how frustrating and time-consuming it can become. This book aims to show how to keep the 'hassle-factor' to a minimum and achieve a positive, speedy outcome. It has been specifically written for those faced with a consumer problem, and for all who wish to adopt a firmer stance in their general everyday transactions.

More and more people are – quite rightly – forgoing the 'stiff upper lip'. Why should shoddy goods and services be tolerated? If you don't complain, how will things ever improve? There are recent new initiatives to help those who have a grievance. This book considers useful alternatives, as well as the traditional approaches to resolving any dispute. There is no need to suffer in silence. There is no need to suffer at all.

Having read this book, it is hoped that you will feel more confident in your dealings as a consumer and that, if you need justice, you will know where and how to get it.

Is this you?

Shopper   Consumer

                          Signed a contract

In business   Buying on credit

                              Householder

Student   Policyholder

                          Member of the public

Freelancer   Subcontractor

                        Citizens Advice Bureau

Solicitor   Rights adviser

                               Law centre

Purchaser   Paid a deposit

                                 Retailer

Young person   Business manager

                          Professional adviser

Debt counsellor   Taxpayer

                        Trading Standards Officer

Customer   Client

                          Credit card holder

Bank borrower   Mortgagor

                          Insured against loss

1
Knowing Your Rights

EFFECTIVE COMPLAINING

Do you want to complain and win? This book tells you how. For effective complaining you need to know:

- your rights
- the techniques
- the action.

As a consumer, more types of remedies are opening up to you. New law protects you in entering any contract and the courts are no longer the only place to take your grievance. There are choices like ombudsmen and a developing range of other so-called 'alternative dispute resolution'. All this will help you – quickly and cheaply – to get what you want.

This book covers your main options. It steers you through the procedure towards the right solution for you.

LIVING UNDER THE LAW

Like it or not, you live under a large legal umbrella. Used correctly, it can offer you much shelter from the problems arising in everyday life.

The complex regulations which mushroom underneath that simple, three-letter word – 'law' – are endless. Many will have limited impact on you and can be left to the academics and specialists. A select few fall within the structure of everyone's life. Knowledge of these can assist you to avoid or solve disputes at minimum cost.

New developments

You will find this especially so now that effective action is becoming more user-friendly. One example is that the limits in the small claims court increased so more cases can be brought there. People are being

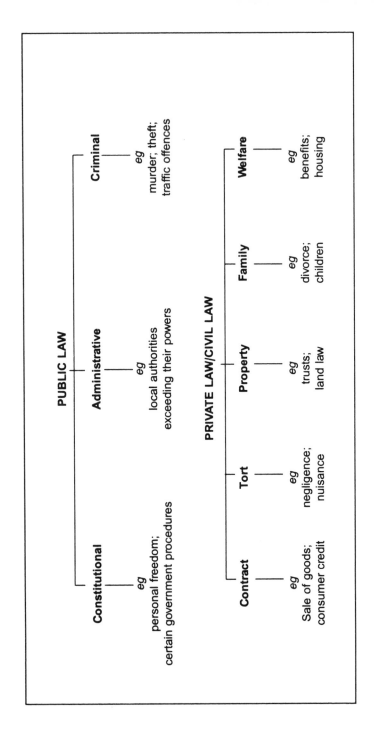

Fig. 1. Types of law.

encouraged to bring cases without having a solicitor or barrister. There has been an expansion in the alternatives to court procedures, many of which are free of charge to you.

> **Addresses are given at the back of this book for organisations which you can contact for help.**

Ignorance of the law is no defence

Whether your grievance is over a faulty garment or being sold an unsuitable mortgage, redress is available. Furthermore, most documents placed before you as a consumer now have to be in plain English. 'Ignorance of the law is no defence' is an old legal cliché. It is also a risk which it is not necessary for you to take.

Types of law

Figure 1 sets out, in broad terms, how the law is broken down into different categories.

Public law may affect you, for example, if you have certain disputes with your local authority. It is, however, private law which concerns most people. Another word for this is **civil law**. This is not used in the sense of 'well-mannered'. (Most private disputes, such as between neighbours, can be very heated – as in the famous case of an irate householder who leapt over a fence to strangle next-door's noisy pet bird.) Civil law really refers to the law which gives you rights you can pursue through the civil courts, such as the County Court or the High Court (see Chapters 4 and 5).

Criminal law on the other hand, is mainly prosecuted by the police/ Crown Prosecution Service, or bodies such as Trading Standards Departments (see Chapter 10). Individuals largely act as witnesses to provide evidence of the crime. Cases are usually heard in the Magistrates Court or Crown Court.

The law relevant to you

This book therefore focuses on civil law, in particular:

- contract
- tort.

These are the basics which are relevant to you as a consumer.

MAKING A CONTRACT

A contract includes any legally binding agreement. Examples are:

- purchase of goods from a retailer
- booking a hotel room
- credit card arrangements
- mortgage agreements.

Certain 'ingredients' are required by law before a contract will be enforceable.

Offer and acceptance

There has to be a deal made. One party offers something which the other accepts. A handshake can symbolise this.

Example

You might offer to sell your car for a price which the buyer accepts. Alternatively the buyer might offer you a smaller amount. This is a **counter-offer** which you may then accept. Either way, there is offer and acceptance.

> **Be warned though – an item which looks like an offer may be regarded in law as just an invitation to treat.**

Major examples of this are price-tags on shop goods. It is you, the customer, who actually makes the offer at the counter when you offer to pay the price stated. The shop accepts and concludes the contract.

Most advertisements are only invitations to treat, but if they are very specifically worded the courts will sometimes see these as offers.

Consideration

This has a different legal meaning to the ordinary one. It is an exchange of promises (or an act in exchange for a promise) worth something to each party.

Example

You agree to hand over your car to the buyer, who agrees to pay you the price.

- Sometimes a promise can be enforced without any consideration being given in exchange for it, through a legal doctrine called **equitable estoppel**, but this can be difficult to establish.

Intention to create legal relations

This is presumed to exist in normal business transactions. If you are dealing commercially with a relative or friend, try to show that you intended everything to be legally binding. Confirming matters in writing can help.

Capacity

In general, you must be over eighteen, sane and sober when you enter a contract (otherwise special rules apply).

Legality

The courts can refuse to enforce any contract which is contrary to legislation or public policy. A contract killing is an extreme example.

Privity of contract

You have to be a party to a contract to enforce it. Third parties cannot usually make claims under it.

Consensus ad idem

This 'lawyers Latin' basically means that there must be agreement without anything to undermine it. One example is that a fundamental mistake about the item which the contract concerns can sometimes render it invalid.

Misrepresentation

This is where you are induced (encouraged) to enter a contract by a false statement of fact made by the other party. It can mean that sometimes you are entitled to **rescind** (undo the contract) and/or claim damages to restore you to your original position.

GETTING IT IN WRITING

A contract need not be set out in a signed written agreement. (There are just a few which must, such as a contract to buy a house.)

Most of the contracts you will make will not be written down, for example those for sale of goods. Even buying a bar of chocolate technically involves a contract. For more important transactions, documentary evidence is a good idea. As the lawyers say, 'A verbal contract is not worth the paper it's written on'.

> To be enforceable, the terms of any contract must be certain. Aim to get conditions spelt out.

Try where appropriate to confirm your dealings in writing. Remember, in particular, the main ingredients required to show a binding contract. Bear these in mind when you are drafting any correspondence. Make sure the terms agreed are clearly stated. Then if the other party lets you down, you are on strong ground to obtain compensation.

BEING 'WRONGED'

If you are the victim of a criminal wrong, you will usually call the police. In some circumstances, you may call a body like a Trading Standards Department (see Chapter 10). In addition to this – or if there is no crime involved at all – you must consider your civil remedies.

The law of **tort** can often help you. 'Tort' is from a French word, and means a civil wrong as opposed to a criminal one (though some acts can amount to both).

Examples of torts
Examples of torts are, in broad terms:

- **negligence** – such as medical negligence or careless driving

- **nuisance** – for example through a neighbour's inconsiderate behaviour

- **trespass to goods** – if someone damages your belongings

- **trespass to land** – where someone enters your property without permission

- **defamation** – where someone speaks slander or writes libel (basically unjustified abuse) about you.

Negligence
The most common and important tort is negligence. It may apply where someone has acted carelessly, causing harm or inconvenience to you. You have to show:

- you were owed a **duty of care** by the person you wish to claim against
- that person has broken the duty of care
- you suffered loss as a result.

To show the first point, you must satisfy the **neighbour test**. This says that there is a duty of care only to those who could reasonably be foreseen as being affected by a certain action (or sometimes failure to take action).

Examples
Case law has indicated that negligence may include:

- a manufacturer making food which causes illness
- the production of clothing which irritates skin
- a doctor making an incorrect diagnosis
- a surgeon leaving a surgical implement inside a patient
- a faulty lock on a public toilet which 'imprisons' the user.

The main example, however, arises with road accidents. Claims (whether or not settled by insurers) are invariably based on the negligence of a road user. If the party to blame is also convicted of a road traffic offence on the same facts, then the claim will usually be watertight.

Overlap with contract claims
You may find that your circumstances amount to both a breach of a contract and negligence.

Someone who, for example, manufactures then sells a faulty product to you could be liable for negligence and breach of contract. If so, it is usually better to rely on your contract claim. This is because **damages** (compensation) for breach of contract may be larger. Contractual damages are meant to place you in the same position as if the contract was carried out. This means they can include items like loss of profit. Damages for tort are only to restore you to the position before the wrong occurred.

CASE STUDIES

Sample situations will be covered throughout this book. They all involve common problems in which the law is illustrated on a practical level. Many are based on real events and legal cases which have arisen in the past.

Whilst neither the case studies nor any other information in this book can foresee and cover specific circumstances which may apply to individuals, they hope to give you several useful pointers.

'Shake on it'

Alan is looking for a car and responds to a private advertisement in the local newspaper. This states a price of '£3,500 O.N.O.'. He tries out the car with the owner, Paul, whom he sounds out on price. Paul indicates that he is willing to take £3,250. Alan replies, 'Say £3,000 and it's a deal.' They shake hands. Alan pays a cash deposit. Paul hands over a written receipt, headed with the registration number, make and model of the car, which reads:

> 'Received the sum of £100 as deposit on sale agreed at a price of £3,000'.

Alan returns a few days later with the balance. Paul explains that he has today been approached by another buyer who will pay £3,250. He hands back Alan's deposit. Alan is fuming.

Alan should put pressure on Paul to conclude the sale to him, by showing a binding contract. The actual advertisement was only an invitation to treat. Paul's indication that he would accept £3,250 would have been an offer, but Alan counter-offered anyway with £3,000, which Paul accepted. There was legal consideration in the exchange of promises to sell/pay for the car. Intention to create legal relations will be presumed here, and there is no problem with any other contractual requirement.

The receipt is the vital evidence for the contract. Alan should make it clear that he will hold Paul to this and that, unless he is allowed to take the car, will be looking for compensation, including any extra cost in buying a similar car.

Barbara is wrongly assessed

Barbara is a self-employed hairdresser who in 1996 receives an estimated assessment from the Inland Revenue for the previous tax year. She forwards this to her accountant. In past years, he has always appealed against any assessment, applied for postponement of the tax assessed and subsequently submitted her accounts, together with calculation of the correct tax due. This particular year, he slips up and does not appeal within the time limit. As a consequence, Barbara receives a demand for the original amount of tax stated, which is well over what she has paid before.

Barbara has a possible claim against the accountant for negligence. If the IR refuse to allow a late appeal and the tax has to be paid in full, she could claim any extra above the correct amount from the accountant. He would very likely be covered by professional indemnity insurance. This means that insurers may reimburse her rather than the accountant himself (depending upon his excess clause).

Failing the deadline

Mr and Mrs Robinson purchase a seaside property to renovate and use as a small guest house.

They consult a builder, who gives them general guidance, draws up the plans, obtains planning permission/building regulations approval and gives an all-inclusive quotation for the work involved. They accept this and, based on the builder's estimates, stipulate a strict deadline in writing for the work to be completed in time for the next summer season. By the following autumn, the work is still unfinished.

The Robinsons may have a claim in negligence. They could argue that the builder owed them a duty of care as regards the advice and expectations they were given. However, they may have a much stronger claim for breach of contract, through failing the written deadline. The contractual claim would potentially include loss of profit for business lost over the summer, which a claim in tort could not.

SUMMARY

- In any grievance you have, from a minor retail transaction to a complex financial one, there is likely to be an effective remedy.

- Addresses of organisations which may be able to help you, are listed in the back of this book.

- The branches of civil law most likely to give you useful rights are contract and tort.

- To show a binding contract exists, always get agreements confirmed in writing.

- Aim to have this written confirmation refer to the terms of the offer, acceptance, consideration and legal relations involved.

- The tort of negligence is often relevant and applies when someone fails in a duty of care towards you causing you loss.

- If you have contractual rights in a situation, these are usually the ones primarily to rely upon, rather than rights in tort.

DISCUSSION POINTS

1. Think of examples of agreements you have made. Which of these can amount to binding contracts?

2. As regards the people you come across in daily life, which do you feel owe you a duty of care so that you are not adversely affected by their actions?

3. Suppose you purchase a house aiming to improve it and enhance its value. On moving in, you discover widespread evidence of damp not disclosed in the survey. What sort of claim/s could you have?

'...remember to read the small print...'

2
Giving 'Chapter and Verse'

STATING YOUR CONSUMER RIGHTS

The ground you have covered in Chapter 1 leads to many specific rights, useful to you, as a consumer.

Figure 2 gives a table of major legal provisions, with examples of situations when you might be able to rely upon them.

USING SALE OF GOODS ACT LAW

The customer is always right

Sale of Goods legislation is generally consumer-friendly. It supports your position in purchasing goods or services or a combination of both. There are several main statutes.

- Sale of Goods (Implied Terms Act) 1973
- Sale of Goods Act 1979
- Supply of Goods and Services Act 1982
- Sale and Supply of Goods Act 1994.

What's it all about?

The cornerstone of the legislation is really the Sale of Goods Act 1979. There has been a Sale of Goods Act around in one form or another for over a century. The 1979 Act consolidated and updated the law, and was then itself updated by the Sale and Supply of Goods Act 1994. As you may have guessed, these laws relate to the sale of items, such as food, toys, cosmetics, clothing, furniture and vehicles.

The Supply of Goods and Services Act 1982, on the other hand, concerns (as you might expect from the name) contracts for the supply of services and work done together with any materials/items supplied. An example might be if you had your home re-roofed. The builder supplies roof tiles and other materials, in addition to his labour. This Act also covers the hire of equipment, such as cars or TV. It does not include hire purchase (HP), because this is covered by the Supply of Goods (Implied Terms) Act 1973.

SOURCES OF RIGHTS	EXAMPLES WHERE APPLICABLE
Sale of Goods legislation	Buying products over the counter, by mail order, or on hire-purchase. Obtaining services.
Consumer Protection Act 1987	Suffering illness, injury or loss through a defective product.
Consumer Protection (Cancellation of Contracts Concluded Away from Business Premises) Regulations 1987	Cancelling a contract within 7 days where a trader visited your home without your request.
Trade Descriptions Act 1968 (see Chapter 10)	Discovering that goods or services are falsely described.
Consumer Credit Act 1974	Purchasing on credit (in various forms including credit cards).
Unfair Contract Terms Act 1977	Exclusion clauses (for example 'get-outs' in holiday terms and conditions).
Unfair Terms in Consumer Contracts Regulations 1994	Standard contracts you are asked to sign, for example small print conditions in a mortgage.
Package Travel, Package Holidays and Package Tour Regulations 1992	Buying package holidays.
The Timeshare Act 1992	Can give you a 'cooling-off' period to change your mind when you buy a timeshare – but applies largely to buying in the UK. (There are plans to extend this to most of Europe by April 1997).

Fig. 2. Table of provisions.

24

What can these laws can do for you?

The basic aim of these statutes is to **imply** terms – **in your favour** – in relevant contracts. This means that you do not have to expressly state such provisions. The seller cannot usually restrict these, such as through a 'No refunds given' notice.

So what can you expect?

The general terms implied for your benefit as a consumer, are:

- that the seller has the right to sell the goods

- that the goods correspond with their description

- that goods sold by sample will be like the sample

- that goods are of **satisfactory quality** (where sold in the course of a business)

- that goods are reasonably fit for any purpose you made known to the seller (who sold in the course of a business) – unless you did not rely on his skill and judgement or it was unreasonable to do so.

(It can be different for sales by auction.)

Similar conditions apply when you obtain goods under an HP agreement, a contract for hire (like a rental agreement) or other contract for the supply of goods. One example could involve a contract for work and materials, such as if a garage fitted spare parts whilst servicing your car.

The conditions also apply to most part-exchange arrangements.

Service, please!

You may also order services, ranging from visiting a restaurant to employing interior designers to re-style your home.

If any items delivered under such contracts are defective, for example faulty curtain rails, then they are usually covered by the type of conditions already mentioned and have to be of satisfactory quality. What if the curtains themselves have been badly made? Services provided in the course of a business have a separate implied term that:

- they will be done with reasonable care and skill
- and within a reasonable time (where no specific time has been stated)
- with a reasonable price paid for them (where no set price has been agreed).

How good is satisfactory?

Your right to expect goods of satisfactory quality could be useless if it was so vaguely interpreted as to cover nothing. On the other hand, too tight a definition might unfairly rule out some possibilities. The legislation therefore gives an indication of what is included, but every case is looked at on its own circumstances.

- Goods are of satisfactory quality if they meet the standard which a reasonable person regards as satisfactory, taking account of any description, the price and all other relevant circumstances.

(The old terminology of 'merchantable' quality was replaced from 3 January 1995 with 'satisfactory'.)

The reasonable person

What is satisfactory is therefore **objective**. It depends upon a reasonable person's expectations.

The law often uses 'reasonableness' as a test (as you will see throughout this book). The hypothetical reasonable person has been seen as someone without eccentric likes and dislikes – the proverbial 'man on the Clapham omnibus'.

Quality not quantity

Relevant to deciding whether an item is of satisfactory quality, are:

- state and condition
- fitness for usual purposes for which that type of thing is commonly supplied
- appearance and finish
- freedom from defects
- safety
- durability.

Sold as seen

You cannot complain of unsatisfactory quality due to a defect drawn to your attention when you purchased. This often occurs in sales, where stickers mark flaws in garments.

You get what you pay for

This does not mean that you cannot complain over sale goods or those on special offer – or even sold in a second-hand shop. The price is relevant to what quality you can expect, but just because goods are discounted does not exclude your rights.

You cannot complain over unsatisfactory quality for any defect which you spotted when you examined goods before purchase, or if you should have spotted it in your examination. The same applies if you purchase by sample.

Beware acceptance

If you 'accept' sub-standard goods, you lose your right to reject them later. You can still claim damages (money compensation), such as cost of repair. You will be stuck with the defective item, rather than being able to return it and claim a full refund and/or damages.

What amounts to 'acceptance'?

The main examples are:

Intimating to the seller that you accept the goods (provided you had reasonable opportunity to examine them).

This could be, for example, by letter expressing your satisfaction.

Signing a **delivery note** is unlikely to amount to 'acceptance', even if the note says that you acknowledge receipt in good condition, because a consumer usually has the right to prior inspection.

Doing an act relating to the goods inconsistent with the ownership of the seller (provided you had reasonable opportunity to examine them).

This could occur, for example, in certain circumstances where you sell the goods to someone else, or use them as raw material to make into something else.

Allowing reasonable time to pass without intimating to the seller that you reject the goods.

This is the most common and trickiest 'acceptance'. What is 'reasonable time' depends on the circumstances in each case. It is not generally reasonable to take packaged food back after the sell-by date. The less perishable and more expensive an item, the more likely it will merit a longer 'reasonable time'.

The buyer of a new car tried to reject it, after its first run following purchase. He had owned it for scarcely three weeks, including Christmas and whilst he was ill. Nevertheless, the court held that reasonable time had passed. Some recent provisions may help alleviate such situations – but the warning is clear. **Act quickly**.

In deciding the reasonable time, however, account is taken of what opportunity was available to examine goods. This may help someone who shops in the January sales for birthday presents to give them still packaged throughout the year.

To be on the safe side:

- check purchases as soon as practicable
- raise any complaint without delay.

In complaints over supply of goods and services, there is no acceptance, but you can lose your right to reject if you **affirm** the contract. This can be by treating it as still in existence once you know about the fault. Again time lapse can be critical. Raise any complaint as promptly as possible.

Questions and answers

Do you have more protection buying from a shop than buying privately?

You have more rights when buying from a shop. Basically when you buy privately, goods only have to be 'as described'.

What is the difference between a quotation and an estimate?

Normally a quotation is the price you would expect to pay later, whereas an estimate is more an indication in the region of the final price. Often, however, the two terms are used interchangeably. Both provide good evidence of what the 'reasonable price' should be, if a dispute develops.

Do I have to accept a credit note when returning goods to a shop?

If the implied conditions are not satisfied, you are usually entitled to replacement or your money back or cost of repair. **You do not have to accept a credit note.** You may have to prove when and where you bought the goods, usually by producing the receipt. If this is lost, try something else like a credit card voucher.

RELYING ON OTHER CONSUMER PROTECTION

Other consumer legislation can also help you, in addition to your Sale of Goods Act rights.

Consumer Protection Act 1987

This says there is **strict liability** (*ie* responsibility even where a person/company did not make or contribute to any defect) for damage caused to anyone or damage caused to private property exceeding £275 through any defect in goods supplied by:

- the manufacturer/producer
- an importer into the European Union
- an 'own brander'.

So if you suffer personal injury from defective goods, or property damage over £275 you can claim.

If any supplier in the distribution chain fails to identify those listed above or his own supplier, then he also can be liable. This is to prevent you losing out simply because you are unable to identify the person or organisation against whom the claim can be brought.

Sometimes, however, your claim can fail if defences apply, such as 'state of the art'. In general terms, this is when the supplier can show that the state of scientific and technical knowledge was not such that a producer could reasonably have known about those defects.

This act created several criminal offences which can catch suppliers. (see Chapter 10.)

Trade Descriptions Act 1968

This can apply if you purchase goods, facilities or services which you then find have been falsely described (see Chapter 10).

Consumer Credit

The Consumer Credit Act 1974 (with additional regulations) has been brought slowly into force over about twenty years, which gives some idea of its complexity and volume.

Consumer credit can cover many credit transactions including:

- HP
- conditional sale agreements
- credit sales
- loans (secured and unsecured)
- credit card accounts
- budget shop accounts
- overdrafts.

There are some exemptions. To be within the main provisions, the credit has to be generally for under £15,000. The provider of the credit is required to be licensed.

The legislation aims to protect you, the consumer. Your rights should usually be stated clearly in the literature you receive on signing any credit agreement. These include **the right to cancel** in certain circumstances. For example, if you have been sold something on credit during a representative's visit to your home and soon after you regret falling for the hard-sell.

You may also later have **the right to terminate** the agreement. This is more of a last resort, but can help if you are struggling financially to keep up payments. You may have to pay up to one-third of the total price, as well as returning the goods.

If you default on payments and the creditor serves a **default notice**, you can apply to the court for a **time order** to allow more time to pay.

Lost credit tokens
If you lose for example a Visa card, and it is misused by someone else, your liability should not usually exceed £50.

Creditor's liability
There are some interesting provisions which technically allow a claim for breach of contract to be brought against the credit supplier as well as the seller, usually in certain circumstances where the price involved is between £100 and £30,000. (This law may soon be modified.)

It's extortionate!
You can apply to court for an extortionate credit bargain to be examined and altered. This is aimed at credit sharks, and has only been used in a few cases involving very high interest rates.

ARE YOU ON FAIR TERMS?

Suppose you are unhappy with a particular arrangement but cannot walk away from it because there is a binding contract. The law may still be able to alleviate your situation if the terms are unfair.

Unfair Contract Terms Act 1977
This may sound like the answer to all your problems, but the name of the Act is misleading.

It does not cover all contract terms – just mainly **exemption (or exclusion) clauses**. These try to prevent liability (mainly arising in the course of a business) for contract or tort claims. An example might be a holiday contract which states that no claims will be accepted for failure to provide the stated accommodation. Clauses which allow change to fundamental matters promised by a contract can also be affected.

The act also applies to notices. One example is the type you often see on car-park walls, denying responsibility for damage and stressing that 'parking is at the owner's risk'. Sometimes such provisions are not in the contract anyway. Court cases indicate that, to be incorporated in the contract, they have to be brought to your attention at an early stage. (One judge suggested a red hand symbol should point to the wording, to alert people to it.) The provisions have to be very clearly worded. Any ambiguity will normally be interpreted in your favour.

In broad terms, any attempt to exclude liability for claims for death or personal injury, or claims under the implied Sale of Goods Act terms, are void. (It can also be a criminal offence to put such clauses in a consumer sale of goods or HP contract.)

As regards other claims, such as for damage to property caused by negligence, an exclusion will only be valid if it is **reasonable**.

When is it reasonable?
It depends on circumstances but the courts can take into account inequality of bargaining power. The burden of proving the clause is reasonable is on the party relying upon it – usually your opponent.

Example
One case concerned lost wedding photographs. The company who processed them attempted to rely on a printed clause on an envelope limiting its liability to a replacement film. This was unreasonable.

The Unfair Terms in Consumer Contracts Regulations 1994
Many a bank, building society, insurance company and other large organisation has rushed to re-draft its standard documentation as a result of these (which came into force on 1 July 1995 following a European Directive). This is because **any term found unfair under the regulations will not bind you as a consumer**, with the rest of the contract valid only if it can continue without this term. This has been quite an incentive for businesses to get it right.

The regulations primarily apply to standard form/'small print' conditions *ie* any term **not individually negotiated**.

There is an exception for **core provisions** which are terms in **plain intelligible language** which define the main subject of the contract or relate to the adequacy of the price or remuneration. There are other exceptions. The regulations do not apply to such as employment contracts.

The regulations say that an unfair term is one which is contrary to the requirement of **good faith** and causes a **significant imbalance in the parties' rights and obligations** under the contract to the detriment of the consumer. In other words, the regulations are on the side of the underdog.

Unfairness depends upon the circumstances in each case, including:

1. bargaining strength
2. any inducement given to you to agree to the term
3. whether the goods/services were supplied to your special order
4. how equitably (fairly) the seller/supplier dealt with you.

Examples of unfair terms:

- saying you must pay compensation out of all proportion, for failing to fulfil an obligation

- allowing the seller/supplier to keep money if you cancel, but not allowing you to do so if he cancels

- including something to bind you to terms which you had no real opportunity to consider

- allowing the seller/supplier to alter terms without a valid reason

- allowing the seller/supplier to alter unilaterally (without your consent) the type of goods or services he will give.

According to previous indications given by the Department of Trade and Industry, a term will not be fair just because you took legal advice on the contract.

Plain English
A consumer contract has to be in plain intelligible language. Otherwise, if there is doubt over its meaning, it will usually be interpreted in your favour.

Although the need for plain English may present a challenge to many lawyers, it is a great relief for the consumer.

Example

Potentially someone who risks losing their home under a repossession clause in the mortgage document might be able to challenge this by:

- writing to the lender stating that the clause (being in a contract dated after 30 June 1995) is unfair under the regulations
- arguing this through the courts (see Chapters 4 and 5)
- implementing a complaint to the Office of Fair Trading
- taking a complaint to the appropriate ombudsman (see Chapter 8).

The Director-General of Fair Trading may, if he considers a term unfair, bring proceedings for an injunction (an order to stop or compel someone to do something) against anyone using that term. However, complaints have to be brought to him. He cannot seek out unfair terms by himself.

Dealing with overlapping claims

The Unfair Contract Terms Act and the Unfair Terms in Consumer Contracts Regulations work alongside each other. Sometimes both can apply. The Act will probably give you better protection than the regulations in some situations. However the Act does not apply as widely as the regulations (for example, insurance contracts are excluded from the Act). The Act is primarily concerned with reasonableness, but the regulations govern unfairness, with emphasis upon use of plain English.

Problems of overlap may arise. As the regulations are still fairly new, only time and future case law will show their exact implications.

CASE STUDIES

'I want my money back'

Shalika buys a washing-machine with a twelve-month guarantee. It works fine for a day but then she finds that it is not spinning as it should. She rings the shop where she purchased it. They say that it sounds like a simple problem and send someone out to make an adjustment, but there is no improvement. Shalika is told that she must now contact the manufacturer.

Shalika can contact the manufacturer, or insist that the shop resolve her problem by replacing the machine or taking it back and giving her a refund. Under the Sale of Goods Act, the machine must be of satisfactory quality and fit for its purpose. Strict liability is placed upon the seller. Shalika has not accepted the goods at this stage, merely by agreeing to a repair under an arrangement with the seller.

If it had been a few months since Shalika bought the machine, then she might have accepted it and forfeited her right to reject. The guarantee could then be very useful to her. The manufacturer has to honour this, as a guarantee is usually seen by the courts as something known as a **collateral contract**, ancillary to the contract between the buyer and seller.

A 'botched' job

Ray accepts a quote from a company to instal central heating. The quotation includes a small print clause stating:

> The company accepts no liability and gives no guarantee as to the suitability of material supplied or fitted; nor responsibility for any loss, defect or damage arising.

Upon completion of the work, Ray pays in full. However, two weeks later, several radiators start to leak, ruining a carpet.

Ray has entered a contract for work and materials to which the Supply of Goods and Services Act is relevant. Conditions are implied that materials will be of satisfactory quality and fit for the purposes for which they are commonly bought, as reasonable in the circumstances. It is also implied that the services (here the installation) will be carried out with reasonable care and skill.

The company are in breach of these conditions. They may try to rely on the exclusion clause to say that they are not liable. Under the Unfair Contract Terms Act, the clause will be void so far as it attempts to exclude liability for breach of satisfactory quality and fitness for purpose implied conditions.

As regards excluding liability for breach of the condition for reasonable care and skill (*ie* negligence), very clear wording is required for this to work. It is doubtful that this clause is specific enough. Even if it is, it has to be reasonable in the circumstances which actually were, or ought reasonably to have been, contemplated by Ray and the company when they made the contract. It is unlikely to be reasonable here.

Ray should therefore be able to claim from the company for rectification of the problem and damage to the carpet. Ray is under a **duty to mitigate**, *ie* minimise the cost of his loss. To begin with he may have to allow the company to repair the system, rather than Ray using a new firm. If there were further problems (so that their track record becomes very bad) then Ray might be justified in using someone else instead and holding the company responsible for the cost.

Wishing I wasn't here

Jane books herself and her family on a week's skiing trip through a travel agent. The package is to include flights, accommodation, meals, lift passes and ski hire.

Problems arise from the start. Firstly the holiday is delayed on account of overbooking. The hotel is of poor quality, without many of the facilities stated in the brochure. To cap it all, the ski lifts are broken due to bad maintenance.

Both the travel agency and the tour company are potentially liable for these complaints. (They may have some defence if the problems are shown not to be the supplier's fault.)

In addition to her statutory rights, Jane can base her case for substantial compensation on the package holiday regulations (see Figure 2). These give considerable rights and limit the scope for exclusion by tour operators. They protect the person who actually books and anyone, such as family, on whose behalf the package is purchased.

It can be a criminal offence to supply misleading information relating to the package, and brochures must be legible, comprehensible and accurate. Jane should have no difficulty in getting redress based on these facts. She should report her complaints to any holiday representative at the resort. She may have to complete a standard form. She should also write to the company with full details as soon as possible on her return.

SUMMARY

- In assessing the legal basis of your grievance, first check whether there is a contract.

- If so, decide what type of contract it is, for example sale of goods, HP.

- Pick out the stated terms.

- Consider if there are any implied terms, for example under the Sale of Goods Act.

- Evaluate whether any term has been breached.

- Check there is no *valid* exclusion clause covering the breach.

- Consider whether there could have been acceptance/affirmation.

- If possible, reject the goods and/or claim damages for loss.

- Bear in mind that other legislation may help you, for example the Trade Descriptions Act or the Unfair Terms in Consumer Contracts Regulations.

- Think whether there was any misrepresentation at the outset.

- Consider also whether you could have a claim in tort.

DISCUSSION POINTS

1. Consider the contracts you have entered. Try to classify these, for example sale of goods or supply of goods and services.

2. Identify which terms are implied into these contracts by law.

3. What claims could you make in the event of a breach of these terms?

3
Raising a Complaint

BEING ASSERTIVE AND PERSUASIVE

The method of bringing a complaint can be as important as the content of it – just as the clever presentation of a case in court can be as vital to the verdict as the legal authorities upon which it is based. The way you complain can affect how soon your complaint is resolved and with what outcome.

Voicing your complaint

Complaints frequently commence with a face-to-face situation. This might be when you take a faulty garment back to the shop or visit your bank manager to discuss discrepancies in your statement.

Sometimes a meeting may be suggested at a later stage in your complaint. (Often this may be to 'sound you out' on an offer of settlement.)

Bear in mind the following guidelines in such situations:

- Make sure you have a clear idea of your case, your claim and the outcome you want.

- Remember that impressions count. Look and act business-like. You are less likely to suffer an attempt to fob you off.

- Keep the person in front of you separate in your mind from the issue. Otherwise the situation can become confused and over-personal.

- Be aware of your body language. Stand upright and maintain eye contact.

- Speak in a strong voice, but without shouting.

- Never commence with apologies or negatives like 'I'm sorry to trouble you, but...'.

- State your problem succinctly and make your requested clearly.

- Listen to the response you receive, maintaining eye contact.

- If the response is not on the lines you wanted, make it clear that you wish to proceed to a further stage. This might be through speaking to an employee in higher authority, like the manager or through writing to the head office of the organisation concerned.

- If a compromise is proposed to you, resist responding on an impulse. An alternative is to say that you will consider this and reply within a week.

Figure 3 shows the steps to remember when initiating a complaint.

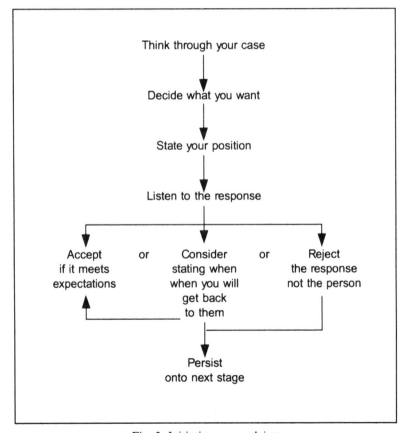

Fig. 3. Initiating a complaint.

USING POSITIVE AGGRESSION

Aggression is often our response when we feel that we have been wronged. The provider of some item or service has let us down – or worse still, duped us into parting with good money for a bad result.

However hard done by you may feel, do not let yourself become a victim of your own emotions. A tirade of invective against the guilty party will not produce the most positive outcome. Remain as calm as you can. Channel your feelings into powering you towards the redress you want. Compensation is worth more in the long run – and vindicates you more – than a situation in which you merely let off steam. In this way you can use your aggression in a positive manner.

HOW TO THREATEN

Management consultants speak of **consequence assertion**, by which they mean a very strong form of assertiveness in which you point out the results of actions to another person. It is not far removed from a polite form of threat. When you bring any complaint, a reference to the 'bottom line' rarely goes amiss.

Examples
1. 'I'm sure we can sort this out. I really hope not to have to resort to court proceedings.'

2. 'It's such a shame that this mistake has occurred. I'm sure your company will want to put it right. I'd rather not have to involve Trading Standards, even though they'd find this situation interesting.'

3. 'Your trade association probably offer arbitration in such matters, but I'm sure we'd both rather avoid that if we can.'

4. 'I understand that your organisation is a member of an ombudsman scheme. I'd prefer not to resort to that, if we can resolve this here and now.'

PUTTING YOUR CASE IN WRITING

Depending on the circumstances, it can sometimes be better to put your case in writing at the outset. It can help you to:

- 'let off heat' in a more coherent format

- itemise your grievances
- formulate your arguments
- specify the redress you require.

Consider using a fax, if available. You may find that this works out cheaper and is more effective than a telephone call. (Often the right person is not at his/her desk and you are kept waiting or are passed around between departments.) You can also state that you expect someone to call you that day to discuss the problem.

Frequently you will have to put any complaint in writing in any event, when initial contact has failed to produce a solution. It is a good idea to address your letter to a particular individual, either by name (if known) or title, for example 'The Customer Relations Manager'. Even if you feel doubtful that your letter will achieve results, it is advisable to send it because:

- it can provide useful evidence later of when your complaint was notified

- it can help rebut any suggestion of acceptance/affirmation (see Chapter 2)

- many complaints schemes require this (an ombudsman will not usually investigate until deadlock is reached – see Chapter 8)

- if you sue, you are unlikely to get costs awarded unless you can show you gave an opportunity to reach a solution before taking proceedings.

Getting it all down

Aim to make your letter **comprehensive but compact**. List all the items about which you are complaining. Avoid digressing into the irrelevant or including too much background detail which will not affect the outcome. A short succinct letter often packs the most punch.

Follow these guidelines for your draft:

(a) Summarise the relevant facts.

(b) State your complaint(s).

(c) Include brief reference to any law which you feel supports your case.

(d) Enclose copies of any documentary evidence which backs you up such as correspondence or receipts.

(e) If there are witnesses who will corroborate (back up) what you say, stress this fact.

(f) Set out the redress you seek, for example reimbursement of expenses.

Example
Moira and Tim recently sold their flat to move to a larger property, as they are starting a family. They were anxious that the sale should proceed with all speed.

Unfortunately this objective was put at risk when their solicitor found difficulty in obtain the title deeds. These were being stored by the building society with whom they had a mortgage and – it seems – had been 'misplaced'. Their solicitor spent a great deal of time chasing the society to locate and release the deeds, which it finally did after several weeks.

Figure 4 sets out the form which an initial letter of complaint might take in this matter.

Who to contact
Such a letter would be addressed to the first point of contact – here the branch manager.

When you put your complaint in writing it will usually be to the seller or supplier of the item/service involved in your complaint at the business address from where it was sold/supplied.

Consider whether you should also write, either at this stage or later if it proves necessary, to other relevant parties. These might include:

- the seller/supplier's head office
- any manufacturer
- any trade association of which the seller/supplier is a member
- your local Trading Standards Department (see Chapter 10)
- any relevant ombudsman's office (see Chapters 8 and 9)
- consumer bodies (see Chapter 7)
- the media.

CASE STUDIES

Bull in a china shop
In the middle of a business meeting, Elaine realises that she has forgotten her mother's birthday. She rushes out in her lunch-break to buy a certain figurine, as her mother collects these. During the afternoon, she looks again at the figurine and finds that she hates it.

For the attention of the Branch Manager

Dear Sirs

<u>Mortgage account number: 1234567</u>

As you may be aware, we recently encountered great difficulty in obtaining the release of the title deeds to our property. Furthermore, this occurred at a crucial stage in the proposed sale.

Our solicitor first requested the deeds on 14 March 199X. Despite several subsequent letters and telephone calls, these were still not despatched until 10 May 199X i.e. some two months later. This delayed preparation of a draft contract by our solicitor and temporarily put at risk the whole transaction. To date, no satisfactory explanation has been received.

We hold the society responsible for this delay, which we believe demonstrates the breach of a duty of care. As a result, our legal costs were larger than they would otherwise have been. We enclose a copy of a letter from our solicitor confirming the position. We therefore seek a contribution of £100 towards legal costs to reimburse us for this extra expense. We feel sure that you will also appreciate the distress and inconvenience caused to us. We would therefore ask the society to make a gesture towards compensation in this respect, in the sum of £200.

In the event that you are not able to resolve our complaint on the lines we suggest, we would ask you to put this matter through your internal complaints procedure forthwith. Whilst we hope that it will not be necessary, we shall consider taking the matter to the Building Societies Ombudsman, or taking other action.

We look forward to hearing from you within the next seven days.

Yours faithfully

Fig. 4. Letter of complaint.

What's more there is a small crack at the base. She also discovers that, in her haste, she has chosen the wrong make of pottery.

Elaine returns with the item and receipt just as the shop is closing and demands to be allowed to select an alternative or be given a refund. The assistant has a bus to catch and suggests that Elaine returns tomorrow. As Elaine is seeing her mother that night, she refuses and asks where the correct range is located. The assistant explains that they have none in stock, at which Elaine becomes very angry and accuses her of being deliberately unhelpful. The shop assistant calls the security guard.

Elaine has approached the situation badly, mainly due to time pressures of her own making. She may not have properly explained her complaint to the assistant. She has no right to a replacement or a refund simply because she bought the wrong type of figurine, or because she has now decided that she doesn't like it. Exchange or refund is then totally at the retailer's discretion, unless for example she had been given any assurance as to the make. The fault in the pottery does however mean that she can ask for a replacement or refund. She should have stressed this aspect to the assistant. Allowing the scene to become emotional has not helped Elaine make her point or obtain what she wants.

Prove it!

A local high street dry-cleaners has a 'Two for the Price of One' offer advertised in the window. James takes in two suits for dry-cleaning. He picks them up later in the week.

Examining them at home, James finds that one has been stained with some form of chemical. Checking his receipt, he also finds that he has been charged full price. He returns to the shop with the suit. The assistant explains that the offer was never intended to apply to suits. She also maintains that the stains could not have been caused by the cleaning process. James is firm but well-mannered and asks to see the manager. He is told that the manager is away for a few days.

James decides to write a letter marked for the manager's urgent attention on his return. James sets out the circumstances and that he requires a refund of the amount which he feels he has overpaid, together with compensation for the ruined suit. He mentions that if this matter cannot be resolved, then he intends to contact Trading Standards over the advertised offer. As regards the stains, he states that he dislikes having his integrity doubted, but will consider having the matter checked by the Textile Services Association and referring it for arbitration to any trade association, to which the dry-cleaners belong.

The manager returns from a training course to a backlog of correspondence, including James's letter. Unbeknown to James, the company has previously had problems with Trading Standards over misleading advertisements and is anxious to avoid prosecution or adverse publicity on this. The manager is also loathe to spend administrative time on a trade association arbitration.

The manager telephones James a few days later and offers a reasonable sum of money to settle the matter. James accepts this as it covers the cost of the suit and the amount by which he felt overcharged, plus an additional amount for goodwill.

Good practice

Simon receives his monthly bank statement and finds that his balance is less than expected, due to a debit entry for charges.

He telephones his local branch to query the statement. The clerk there informs him that the charges are in line with the bank's normal tariff and relate to certain cheques which were returned unpaid when there were insufficient funds in the account to meet them. Simon protests that he did not know that charges would be made, and that the situation had arisen owing to an unexpected delay in his salary being paid that month. He says that he was under the impression that the account attracted 'free banking'. The clerk has no authority to waive the charges.

Simon writes to the branch manager, objecting to the charges, setting out the circumstances and his lack of knowledge of any charges.

Under the Code of Good Banking Practice, banks must act fairly and reasonably towards customers. The basis of any charges applicable to an account should be provided in advance. This can be through standard leaflets given or sent to customers when accounts are opened or at any time on request. The details should also be available in branches. Customer should also usually be given fourteen days' notice of any amount to be deducted from their accounts for charges.

Here the branch manager feels that it is doubtful that Simon was ever properly notified of the charges to apply. He writes back to Simon confirming that the charges have been removed from the account and enclosing details of those charges which will apply in future.

SUMMARY

- When making a complaint, prepare your case in advance.

- Be assertive and well-mannered.

- State clearly and succinctly your arguments and the redress you require.

- Mention the steps which you will consider taking if the matter is not resolved.

- Follow this up, if necessary, by writing with your complaint to a senior person in the organisation.

- Consider further recourse to court, any manufacturer, trading association, ombudsman, Trading Standards, consumer body and/ or the media.

DISCUSSION POINTS

1. Taking the common situation of returning faulty goods to a retailer, list the ways in which such a situation can be handled effectively so as to obtain an immediate solution to any problem.

2. How might you deal with the situation where you have a valid complaint, but the employee whom you approach is belligerent and uncompromising?

3. Suppose you were in Simon's position in the third case study. Draft a brief letter of complaint to the bank manager.

4
Suing in the Small Claims Court

DECIDING TO BRING A SMALL CLAIM

Suppose you have tried an initial approach and given an opportunity for a reasonable proposal to be made to you. Yet it has still come down to 'See you in court'.

Should you commence proceedings?

For many people, the thought of court involvement conjures up a fear of the unknown worse than anything in *The X-Files*.

You must remember that the **small claims court** is designed not to intimidate. If you feel that you have a good case within its financial limits, then you should certainly consider action through this.

Preliminary considerations

First, check that no time limits prevent you (see Chapter 5).

Secondly, as all lawyers stress, there is no point in suing '**a man of straw**'. In other words, you need to be reasonably confident that the person or organisation which you wish to sue is good for the amount which you claim.

There are some ways of trying to check on the defendant's means, but you must bear in mind that they may involve expense, which you are unlikely to be able to recover.

Examples are:

- a search of the company's register at Company's House – though accounts filed maybe out of date

- checks through a credit reference agency

- a search at the Land Charges Department can reveal some mortgages or bankruptcy.

(See addresses at the back of this book.)

If you feel that it is worth your while to sue, take heart from a recent National Audit Office report. It found that 70 per cent of those putting their cases through the small claims court found the proceedings either fairly or very cheap, and most claimants obtained judgement in their favour.

What is the small claims court?

It is a special section of the County Court. It can deal with claims **up to £3,000**. (This may soon be raised to £5,000.) If your claim falls within the present limit, you may find it is the answer for you because:

• it is cheaper and quicker than other court proceedings

• there is no need to employ a solicitor or barrister

• the procedure is relatively informal.

The small claims court can deal with many consumer disputes. Mainly it hears disputes concerning contract and tort (see Chapter 2). Examples are:

- claims for debts owed
- claims over defective goods
- claims over bad services
- claims for the return of property.

Perhaps you are not yet sure that you wish to follow through any court procedure to the bitter end. You may find that just taking initial steps may 'encourage' a more productive response from the other side.

SENDING A LETTER BEFORE ACTION

This is the first stage. The 'action' in question is court action. This letter represents the last warning shot before involving the court.

Although it is not a set legal requirement, if you do not send such a letter, you are less likely to be able to claim fees and expenses from the other party if you win. It is a good idea to send it by **recorded delivery**. **Always keep a copy**.

This letter should normally:

• set out your complaint as precisely as possible (see the guidelines for letters of complaint in Chapter 3)

7 Meadow Rise
Keddringham

10 August 199X

The Managing Director
K S Carpets Ltd
2 High Street
Keddringham

Dear Sirs

Re: Contract no. 1893

Thank you for your letter dated 3 August 199X.

It seems clear that, despite previous correspondence, telephone
conversations and the recent visit by your representative, this
matter remains unresolved.

To recap briefly, you fitted a hall carpet at my home on 24 April
199X. An unsightly worn patch has appeared in this after only two
months. In choosing the carpet, I made clear to you that the
purpose was for use in a hallway. I relied upon your skill and
judgement that the one supplied by you would be suitable. It is
clear that it is not of satisfactory quality. Therefore, either you put
forward suitable proposals for a replacement or make arrangements
for a refund, or you leave me no alternative but to sue you in the
small claims court.

Unless I hear from you with proposals on the lines indicated within
fourteen days of the date of this letter, then court proceedings will
be commenced against you without further notice. Such
proceedings will include a claim for costs against you.

Yours faithfully

Joan Lane

Fig. 5. Letter before action.

- state the redress you require

- give a time limit for your demands to be met, failing which you will issue proceedings and claim court costs.

Example

Joan had a new carpet laid in the hall two months ago. Already a patch near the door is looking very worn. She has contacted K S Carpets, who supplied and fitted it. They initially suggested that the carpet needed 'wearing in'. Joan insisted they come and see for themselves.

On a visit by their representative, she is told that such wear is only to be expected in that area. 'After just two months!' Joan remarks. She hears the representative mutter something about 'consumer misuse', when her young son enters the room. A few days later she receives a two-line letter denying liability.

Figure 5 sets out the type of letter before action which Joan might send. (There is no need for her to address the 'consumer misuse' referred to by the representative at this stage. If the company wishes to raise this as a defence to her claim, then it will have the burden of proving this).

COMPLETING A SUMMONS FORM

Suppose the deadline given in your letter before action expires and the silence is deafening. Now you must make the final decision.

Bear in mind the points mentioned at 'Should you commence proceedings'. If you decide to proceed, the first step is to issue a summons.

Contact your local County Court office (see the telephone directory under 'Courts'). You can telephone or pay a visit. They are usually open between 10am and 4pm weekdays. Explain that you are bringing a small claim. Ask for the appropriate forms, plus explanatory leaflets.

Guidelines on the next procedure are given below. If, however, you find that you have any specific queries, do not be embarrassed to ask the court office. The personnel there are generally helpful to **litigants in person**, *ie* people like you who are not represented by a solicitor or other adviser.

Issuing the summons step-by-step

If the time specified in your letter before action has expired and your claim is still outstanding:

County Court Summons

(1)
Plaintiff's
full name
address

(2)
Address for
sending
documents
and payments
if not as above
Ref/Tel no.

(3)
Defendant's
full name
*eg Mr, Mrs or Miss
where known*
and address
Company no.
where known

What the plaintiff claims from you

Brief
description
of type of
claim

Particulars of the plaintiff's claim against you

Amount claimed

Court fee

Solicitor's costs

Total amount

Summons issued on

What to do about this summons

**You have 21 days from the date of the
postmark to reply to this summons**
*(A limited company served at its registered office
has 16 days to reply)*
**If this summons was delivered by hand, you
have 14 days from the date it was delivered
to reply**

You can

* dispute the claim

* make a claim against the plaintiff

* admit the claim and costs in full and offer to pay

* admit only part of the claim

* pay the total amount shown above

**You must read the information on the back of this
form. It will tell you more about what to do.**

Signed
Plaintiff or plaintiff's solicitor
(or see enclosed particulars of claim)

Fig. 6. Summons form. Note: The Court Service have asked readers to note
that, due to special criteria for processing the form used at court offices, the
above is a specimen only and should not be copied for use. Originals are
obtainable from court offices.

1. Obtain from the court office, three copies of the summons form – usually **form N1** for claiming a fixed amount, or form N2 otherwise. (Both are similar.)

2. See figure 6 for the layout of form N1.

3. Complete the sections of this as indicated below. It can be hand-written or typed.

4. Insert your full name and address (**as plaintiff**) and any other address (if different) where you wish court documents/payments to be sent to you.

5. Insert the name and address of the person you wish to sue (as **defendant**).

6. In the box headed 'What the plaintiff claims from you', give a brief description of the type of claim, for example, 'loss caused by faulty workmanship'.

7. Where indicated, insert 'particulars' of your claim. This section must give specific detail of the matter and amount involved. Figure 7 gives an example.

8. In the right-hand column, insert in figures the full amount claimed.

9. Also include the court fee you will have to pay. This will usually be between £10 and £70, depending upon the amount claimed. If you can show hardship, ask the court for a fee exemption/reduction.

10. Return the completed forms to the court, with your cheque for any fee made payable to 'H M Paymaster General'.

The court will then **issue** the summons. It will give notice of this (Form 205A) to you. One copy of the summons will be posted to the defendant, who then has fourteen days to reply.

FOLLOWING PROCEDURE

What happens next depends upon the outcome of the issue of the summons. Figure 8 sets out a diagram of the most common possibilities. It indicates the action which you might then have to take in each case.

Particulars of the plaintiff's claim against you

The claim is for £150 plus £22.50 VAT to cover the cost of repairs to leaking gutters.

The Defendant replaced guttering at my house on 10 March 199X. A few weeks later I noticed that the new guttering was leaking at several joints and contacted the Defendant immediately. He promised to call and repair this, but failed to do so, despite several telephone calls and letters from me reminding him of the matter.

Finally, on 20 May 199X, I arranged for another builder to repair the gutters. I contacted the Defendant on 30 May 199X and asked him to reimburse me for the cost of repairs, but the money has not been paid.

Fig. 7. Sample particulars.

ATTENDING ARBITRATION

Disputed claims for £3,000 or less are automatically referred to arbitration. You will receive details such as time, date, place, time allocated and preparatory steps to take (**directions**) at any preliminary appointment (see Figure 8) or, if one is not held, on form N18A.

What is arbitration?

Arbitration is the term here for a small claims court hearing, as opposed to a full County Court hearing. There are also other sorts of arbitration (see Chapter 7).

Arbitration is less formal and more private than other types of court hearing. The arbitrator is usually the District Judge. You can nominate someone else, but this is really only relevant for very specialised cases.

A claim under £3,000 can sometimes be tried in court instead, if your case is very complex or concerns an important principle. Sometimes you may be required to attend a preliminary appointment before the case reaches arbitration, and such issues can be resolved at this stage.

In advance of arbitration you may have to prepare, within a specified time, a list of relevant documents to send to your defendant (as for 'discovery' – see Chapter 5). The defendant must do likewise. A **Certificate of Readiness** (written confirmation that you are ready) may also be required. Send this to court and request a date for the hearing.

Preparing your case

Many cases are won – not on what is said in court – but through the careful preparation carried out beforehand. This often separates the less able lawyer from the good lawyer. No amount of emotive rhetoric can make up for having your evidence to hand and your arguments well-polished, in order to present your case well.

In an arbitration you are, in effect, the lawyer – your own advocate. You can have a solicitor to act but the small claims court is really for ordinary laymen, like yourself, to act on their own behalf. Therefore, in general **no legal costs can be claimed**, even if you win. Up to £260 may sometimes be awarded for legal advice, but usually only in a claim for an injunction or a similar order. Furthermore no legal aid will be granted, except in exceptional circumstances.

You can arrange for someone else, such as a friend, to represent you *ie* do the talking at the arbitration. (If so, you must complete form Ex 83). Bear in mind though that if any such **lay representative** wants to charge, you will have to pay this, even if you win.

Meeting the burden of proof

You have to be aware that, as plaintiff, the onus of proving your claim is on you. The arbitrator has to decide matters on a **balance of probabilities**. You have to tip that balance. Broadly speaking, you must prove that your allegations have at least a 51 per cent likelihood of being true.

Where's your evidence?

You must produce some tangible evidence to corroborate what you say. Your own testimony (sworn statement at a hearing) is unlikely to be sufficient in the face of a defendant's denials.

What can you do to win?

The exact evidence available to you will depend on the circumstances. It could include:

- contracts and agreements
- receipts and invoices
- copy correspondence
- photographs – such as of defective goods.

Witnesses

If important to your case, you should arrange for witnesses to attend, who can support your version of events or your allegations. Bear in mind though, that you will, at least initially, have to pay any expenses

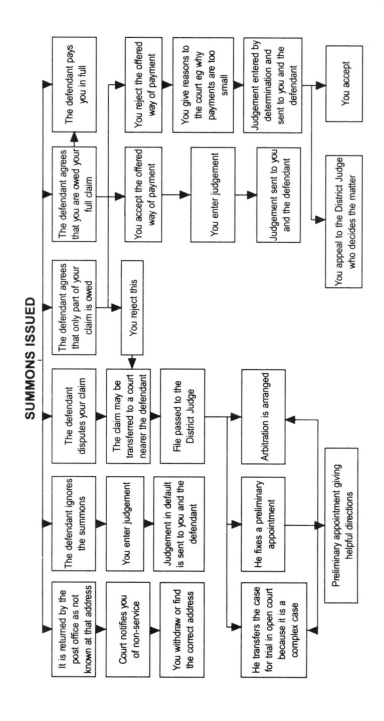

Fig. 8. Some possible routes in a small claim.

requested by these witnesses – especially if you issue a **witness summons** to compel attendance.

Alternatively, you can submit a written statement signed by your witness. However, evidence given in this way may carry less weight.

Expert witnesses
The opinion of someone with specialist knowledge may help your case. You might, for example, obtain a mechanic's report on your car when it was returned from the garage who, you claim, failed to repair it properly. Again you must, at least initially, bear any cost.

Sometimes, up to £200 may be awarded in the small claims court for expert's fees, if you win. Such fees have to be reasonable (not overcharged). They must also be reasonably incurred (justified as necessary).

On the day
- Dress smartly.
- Arrive in good time for the appointment.
- Have all relevant papers and evidence with you, arranged in a clear order.
- Find out from the office/court usher which room the arbitration will be in.
- Meet up with your witnesses (if any) in the waiting room.
- Be prepared to have to wait – sometimes prior cases overrun.

In the arbitration
This will normally take place in a private room at the court. Formality is kept to a minimum – no wigs or gowns, no complex or dramatic terminology, no 'your honour', 'my learned friend', 'submission', 'objection' or 'overruled'.

You must, of course, be polite. Directing abuse at your defendant will generally alienate the arbitrator. Being concise, methodical and efficient in presenting your case will create a good impression.

Address the arbitrator as 'Sir' or 'Madam'. He/she will usually be seated facing you from behind a desk and you will sit on his/her right, with the defendant on his/her left.

Cases are mainly presented and evidence given whilst all parties remain seated. You will be expected to explain your case. Remember to:

- follow a chronological order
- speak clearly but not too quickly (as the arbitrator may wish to take notes)
- be concise.

The arbitrator may query a few points with you. The defendant will also be given an opportunity to question you and your witnesses (if any).

The defendant will be given a chance to speak and have witnesses give evidence. You will then be entitled to pose questions. There is no formal examination/cross-examination process, as in other courts.

The outcome

The arbitrator will consider everything put forward and give his/her judgement (referred to as **an award**). Generally, this is stated at the end of the hearing. Sometimes, the arbitrator may elect to send out a written decision later, to both sides.

If you win, you should normally be entitled to have the defendant pay court fees, reasonable witness expenses and necessary out-of-pocket expenses, in addition to any sums awarded and any interest you have claimed.

If you lose, you can consider an appeal. However, most appeals are only viable on points of law. Cases heard in the small claims court do not usually involve this. The desire to take the matter further is an understandable reaction. However, you may just be throwing good money – not to mention time and effort – after bad.

It is possible that the arbitrator may feel unable to reach a decision. The case may be adjourned (postponed) for a point to be clarified or further information obtained. The arbitrator may find that the case has proved more complex than envisaged and refer it out of the small claims court to the County Court proper (see Chapter 5).

ENFORCING JUDGEMENT

Unfortunately obtaining judgement is not always the end of the story. If your defendant does not pay, you have to move on to **enforcing** the court order.

This is one reason why it is important to decide at the outset that your defendant is worth suing. A recent report suggests that only 58 per cent of plaintiffs have their judgements fully satisfied (get paid in full) soon after. Many must resort to further court procedures.

What options are there?

There are several methods of enforcing a judgement. The main ones are:

- attachment of earnings
- warrant of execution (not as dire as it sounds)
- garnishee order

- charging order
- warrant of possession
- bankruptcy.

Usually a fee has to be paid by you, the amount depending upon the size of the claim. This is then added to the amount owed by the defendant. Which method is most suitable varies according to the debt involved and the financial position of the defendant.

Sometimes it is useful to arrange for the defendant to attend an **oral examination**. You usually need to complete court form N316 for this. At the oral examination, questions are put to the defendant to ascertain income available and capital/assets owned. You can raise your own specific queries. Be as probing as possible, as the court's own enquiries tend to be fairly standard. Examples of questions which you might ask are:

'Do you own a car?'

'Is any money shortly to become due to you?' (Dividends/building society pay-outs/tax refunds could be relevant.)

'Do you own any insurance policies with a surrender value?'

You will probably feel like the Wicked Witch of the West in this situation. Remember though that you are the one whose case has been vindicated by the court. Most defendants try to suggest, 'You can't get blood out of a stone.' This is often just a shield. Persist with all the questions you want to ask.

Which method should you choose?
Study the circumstances in your own case against the criteria outlined below in making your choice.

The alternative PAYE
An attachment of earnings order can be very useful where your defendant is employed as opposed to self-employed.

A sum towards your debt is deducted from the defendant's wages. The debt must be over a certain amount, currently £50.

The court office will give you form N337 to apply for this. The defendant has eight days to respond and pay in full or return a form detailing his finances (failing which he could be in contempt of court and ultimately be imprisoned). A court official determines the amount to be deducted from wages (subject to any appeal to the District Judge). The order is served on the employer who makes the deductions.

Sending in the bailiffs

A warrant of execution sounds like Henry VIII's order for unwanted wives. However it means simply that court bailiffs can take goods belong to the defendant and sell them at public auction to obtain the money due to you. The threat of this action can be very effective.

To instruct bailiffs, complete form N323. If possible, give details of assets which you know that the defendant owns in his sole right. With a car, for example, give the registration number. Some items cannot be taken, such as 'tools of trade'.

The bailiffs will call at the defendant's home to take **walking possession** of the goods. This means that the defendant promises not to dispose of them. If the debt is not paid within an agreed time, the auction goes ahead (subject to application for suspension by the defendant).

If your judgement is for at least £2,000, it may be enforced by you in the High Court, and if over £5,000, it usually is. The advantage is that it always then carries interest. The appropriate document is known as a **writ of fieri facias (fi fa**, for short). Request this on a form called a **praecipe** with the judgement, a sealed certificate of judgement, and two copies of the prepared writ of fi fa.

Direct from the account

Garnishee proceedings are used to take over a debt owed to your defendant. As this can include money in a bank or building society account, this is extremely useful. The procedure is, however, normally only practical for larger debts.

Bricks and mortar

A charging order can be used sometimes where a defendant owns a property. It takes effect similar to a mortgage. Your debt is secured on the property and stands a good chance of being paid from the proceeds of any sale, subject to prior charges.

Apply for this on court form N86, with an **affidavit** (sworn statement – see Chapter 5). The procedure is complex, and only really suitable for larger debts.

(There is also a **warrant of possession**, usually obtained by landlords to evict tenants.)

Pulling the plug

Bankruptcy proceedings (or winding-up in the case of a company) are perhaps the most drastic method. Threat of this can sometimes stir a defendant into paying. However, to carry the procedure through can be costly. If the defendant has no financial assets, you may just rank as one unsecured creditor amongst many, with only the hope of a percentage being paid. Your debt must be over a minimum amount, and this procedure may be more useful for larger claims.

REACHING A SETTLEMENT

If the procedure you have covered here seems daunting, take heart from the fact that most disputes never reach the courtroom. Many are settled before or during proceedings.

You should not therefore be surprised if your defendant – who previously ignored or rejected your claims – suddenly becomes anxious to sort things out. Many businesses wish to avoid a judgement against them, as this can affect their reputation and credit-rating. Risk of bad press is another incentive to settle – not to mention saving time and the cost of court attendance.

If you are approached, remember that it is generally best to negotiate over the telephone or face-to-face, rather than through correspondence. Let the other side mention a figure first, if possible. If it is derisory, reject it. If it is worth thinking about, say you will get back to them, rather than make an impulsive decision. If you have incurred expense, such as a summons fee, ensure this is also included in any amount you agree.

Negotiations should be **without prejudice**. If you receive a written offer, it will probably be headed with this phrase. In general terms this means that if you reject the offer, you cannot later use it in court to prove an admission of fault by the other side. If you accept the offer, any correspondence loses this 'privilege' and can be used to show the agreement for the amount offered. You have then reached a settlement. Sometimes this can be recorded in a written contract, or embodied in a **consent order** by the court. At the very least you should you have it confirmed in writing.

It is in your interests to make clear that negotiations are without prejudice, in case, for example, it could be implied that by entertaining a smaller amount, you admit that your full claim is unjustified.

CASE STUDIES

The circumstances of one claim are considered below in relation to potential outcomes.

Facts

Margaret has purchased a dishwasher. She arranges for the necessary plumbing to be carried out in advance of delivery. When the machine arrives, she follows the instructions. It appears to work well, but at the weekend, a flood of water appears under the kitchen units and causes damage to the floor tiles. Margaret calls her plumber. He finds that a small part in the dishwasher is faulty. He replaces this and stops the leak.

Margaret telephones the shop where she purchased the dishwasher and explains. Their attitude is that it is nothing to do with them and she must contact the manufacturer. She finds it difficult to get beyond the manufacturer's switchboard, and is told that all the manufacturer can do is carry out repairs under the guarantee. Both seller and manufacturer deny liability for the plumber's charges and the cost of any damage.

Scenario 1 – the threat of court
Margaret writes a letter before action to the seller. She gives fourteen days from the date of her letter for a cheque to be sent for the cost of repair and damage. She specifies the total amount clearly, giving a breakdown of how it is made up, and encloses a copy of the plumber's invoice. She states that if the amount is not received in the stipulated time, she will issue proceedings in the small claims court, and claim any court fees incurred.

Margaret receives a cheque the next week, together with a letter of apology from the shop manager.

Scenario 2 – a summons is served
Suppose Margaret's letter before action falls on deaf ears. She obtains and completes the necessary court forms and a summons is issued. After receipt of this, she receives a cheque for the amount of repairs and damage, together with a letter of apology.

Margaret telephones the manager and explains that she cannot accept the cheque in full and final settlement of her claim, nor withdraw her court action, until she receives reimbursement of her court fee. This arrives in the next post. Margaret informs the court office.

Scenario 3 – the matter is disputed
Suppose that, in response to the summons, the retailer indicates that he intends to defend on grounds that the fault was not with the dishwasher, but with the plumbing.

A date is set for arbitration. Margaret takes along copies of all correspondence, notes of telephone conversations and invoices, together with photographs taken of the damage caused. She obtains a brief signed statement from her plumber and brings along the faulty part taken from the machine.

The District Judge listens to both sides. On balance, he is convinced by Margaret's evidence and awards her the sum claimed, together with court fee and out-of-pocket expenses.

Indemnity

In all the above cases, it is likely that the retailer would, behind the scenes, take up the matter with the manufacturer and be entitled to reimbursement from the manufacturer of any amount claimed. (It is also technically possible that the manufacturer could be joined in as a party to the proceedings.)

SUMMARY

- If initial approaches prove unproductive, send a letter before action.

- If your time limit is not met, contact your local County Court office.

- Obtain the necessary forms and leaflets.

- If you are not out of time and confident that your defendant is good for the claim, then issue your summons.

- If your claim is disputed, prepare your case for arbitration.

- Be clear and concise at any hearing.

- If you remain unpaid after judgement, consider a request for an oral examination of the defendant.

- Choose your method of enforcement as appropriate to the amount involved and finances of the defendant.

- If at any time you enter negotiations to reach a settlement, make clear this is without prejudice.

DISCUSSION POINTS

Imagine yourself faced with a similar situation to that in the case study.

1. What wording would you use in your letter before action?

2. How would you present your case step-by-step in a small claims court arbitration?

3. Which methods of enforcement might be relevant if the retailer failed to pay the amount awarded to you?

5
Litigating on Larger Claims

Suing for a larger amount is more difficult – and more financially risky – than using the small claims court. That said, you need not necessarily be deterred. Furthermore, there are changes under way to make the process easier.

SHOULD YOU USE A SOLICITOR?

There are advantages to instructing a solicitor. Against these must be weighed the major disadvantage – cost (see Chapter 6).

If your case is complex, you are well-advised to consult a solicitor. It may be a virtual necessity if you are seeking a special order like a **Mareva injunction** (where you think someone will move assets abroad) or an **Anton Pillar order** (to obtain items such as documents which you think might otherwise be destroyed).

You may feel that using a solicitor will be worth it in the end, or perhaps you are eligible for legal aid. Alternatively, a 'no win, no fee' arrangement might suit your circumstances (see Chapter 6).

A good solicitor can make the difference between win or lose. The other side may also take you more seriously if you are represented. They will be aware that if they lose, they may have to pay your legal costs.

If you decide to use a solicitor, see Chapter 6.

Going it alone
You can act for yourself as a **litigant in person**. The cost of litigation has led to a rise in what the headlines call 'DIY justice'.

Example
A telephone engineer won a five-year battle for possession of his council home. He spent his spare time studying law books and took on a local authority legal team. He won the right to stay with the statutory right to buy, plus costs of approximately £2,000.

Citizens Advice Bureaux estimate the recent increase in litigants in person at 10 per cent. Judges have commented on this trend. One reason may be growing awareness that people on benefit can often start proceedings without paying court fees. Another cause may be cut-backs in legal aid (see Chapter 6). More fundamental may be the realisation that the person who knows and cares most about the case – you – may be able to do the best job.

Lord Woolf in his *Access to Justice* report has suggested civil justice reforms with guiding principles of:

'simplicity, speed, economy and ... certainty of costs'.

This sounds like good news for litigants in person.

The proposals provide for a **fast track** for straightforward, defended cases **between £3,000 and £10,000**, with plans for:

- a maximum of three hours for the trial
- limiting to one expert witness, who gives written not oral evidence
- standard fixed costs.

Emphasis is on reducing expenses and incorporating warnings about cost. This should help avoid the absurdity which sometimes arises, where a plaintiff wins but is virtually out of pocket due to expense. This situation was satirised by the novelist Charles Dickens in *Bleak House*, when the Victorians felt the need for reforms. Things seem to have come full circle to where we need to do so again.

Pilot schemes for alternative dispute resolution (see Chapter 7) are being planned in the Central London County Court as part of the changes. If successful, these schemes will be expanded.

KNOWING THE COURT SYSTEM

The basis of the court system is shown in Figure 9.

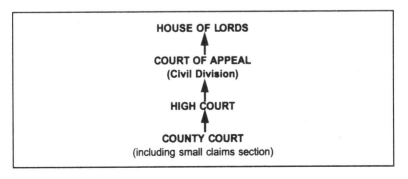

Fig. 9. The civil courts.

Most cases are in the County Court, especially since the **Courts and Legal Services Act 1990** relaxed the amount claimable there. Although you can bring proceedings in the High Court instead, you risk having to pay the extra costs this creates (even if you win), if the judge feels that the County Court was more suitable.

Some claims should be brought in a specific court. The main criteria which generally applies is:

County Court	*High Court*
Actions for personal injuries involving claims for less than £50,000.	Libel and/or slander actions.
	Certain injunctions
Claims for contract or tort not exceeding £25,000.	Judicial review proceedings (see Chapter 7).

Subject to this, any claim you have is more likely to be in the County Court.

Sometimes cases are referred to the High Court, for example, if a complex point of law is involved or if there is an appeal against the County Court decision. The High Court has three divisions:

- Queen's Bench Division
- Chancery Division
- Family Division.

Any consumer complaint in the High Court is likely to be in the Queen's Bench Division, which deals with many matters involving contract and tort.

FOLLOWING PROCEDURE

According to rule

Court procedures are laid down by the *County Court Rules* (CCR). They are contained in a thick volume (not recommended bedtime reading) called the *County Court Practice*. This is known as the *Green Book*, due to its cover. Similar procedures (though often more complex) are contained in the *Rules of the Supreme Court* (RSC), which apply primarily in the High Court. These are found in an equally hefty *White Book*. Some High Court rules also have effect in the County Court. (There are plans to produce simpler rules.)

Court offices have these books and will often allow you to check points. Main libraries usually have reference copies. You will not find either book a gripping read. Much of the terminology may seem obscure. Court staff can help with specific queries. Although they are not able to give legal advice as such, they should be able to assist with the correct forms and procedures.

It is not possible here to summarise all the regulations. One glance in the *Green Book* will tell you why. However, the guidelines which follow will help you to understand the common stages of proceedings.

ISSUING A CLAIM

Taking the plunge

All the points which you covered in Chapter 4 on deciding whether to sue also apply here. In addition, **there is the costs risk**.

Warning – litigation can seriously damage your finances.

The position is different to the small claims court. **You can be ordered to pay the other side's legal costs, which may be very expensive.** This applies whether or not you yourself have employed a solicitor, though it is not usually a risk if you are given legal aid (see Chapter 6) but the position may change.

This is not to say that a person is ordered to write a blank cheque for the other side's expenses. Costs have to be reasonable and reasonably incurred. They can be **taxed** (a procedure which helps check that the expense is justified).

Nevertheless do not underestimate the risk of having costs awarded against you in deciding whether to proceed.

Barred!

You must also check out certain **time limits** before you proceed.

Limitation periods are imposed by statute. These govern how long you are allowed to bring an action, after the event/act happened which is the cause.

A broad summary of the main time limits is:

- for personal injuries arising from negligence, nuisance or breach of duty of care – three years

- for libel and/or slander – three years (though new law may reduce this to one year)

- for certain claims concerning trusts and recovery of land – twelve years (this may also change)

- for most other actions (for example breach of contract) – six years.

Time usually runs from when your **cause of action** (claim) **accrues** – basically when the defendant committed the act (or omission) of which you are complaining.

Often it is not apparent straight away that damage has been caused. One example might be if building faults in your house did not show for several years. The time period is then usually extended to three years after damage became apparent, subject to a maximum of fifteen years, which can be extended in personal injury cases.

Too late

On the subject of timing, you need to be aware that the courts generally look askance on delay. (Do pots and black kettles come to mind?)

The court is bound to be sceptical about your claim if you have 'sat on it' without good reason. Furthermore, if progress in the proceedings is very slow due to you, your action can be **struck out for want of prosecution**.

Before you begin

Always send a **letter before action** before you start proceedings (see Chapter 4).

Issuing the summons

As in the small claims court (see Chapter 4) your action is commenced through issuing a summons. Contact the court office for the appropriate forms.

When suing for a larger claim, it is advisable to heed further formalities, which are less important in the small claims court. Most of these are intended to focus the main issues. They can therefore be helpful – and appreciated by busy judges.

Particulars of Claim

This section of the summons (see Chapter 4 and Figure 7) may be set out in a more formal fashion for a larger claim. Often it is typed on a **separate sheet** usually A4 or foolscap. (Lawyers generally use thicker paper, known as **judicature**, or 'judy' by their secretaries).

An example is set out in Figure 10. This is not intended as a precedent but should give you an idea of the standard structure. Note that the names of court documents like this one usually start with given capital letters. In the documents themselves, words like 'Plaintiff' and 'Defendant' are usually given capitals too.

Although individual circumstances make the criteria vary in each case, the following points may help you in preparing any Particulars of Claim:

• Use numbered paragraphs.

• Keep each paragraph concise.

• Write in the third person, referring to yourself as the 'Plaintiff'.

• In the first paragraph(s), summarise the background to your claim.

• In doing this, state only the **facts** relevant to your case.

• Avoid referring to **evidence**, by which you will prove your case, for example an expert witness report. (This will be put before the court later.)

• In the middle paragraphs, set out your allegations and the law upon which you rely.

• Use one paragraph for each separate allegation.

• Avoid 'pseudo-legalese'. Many laymen make clumsy attempts at this, which can sound pompous. Just use clear and precise language, similar to in a business letter.

• Under a sub-heading '**Particulars**', specify the items you claim, putting a value on any financial loss, where possible.

• If you are claiming for damages for personal injury, you might attach a doctor's report. You do not have to quantify such injuries. They are **general damages** which the court will assess, taking into account usual awards in similar previous cases. (There is a reference book known generally as 'Kemp and Kemp' giving guidelines on such amounts awarded.)

IN THE XMINSTER   Case No:
COUNTY COURT

BETWEEN

                        JOAN LANE   Plaintiff
                         - and -
                D. Z. DECORATORS LIMITED   Defendant

                     PARTICULARS OF CLAIM

1. The Defendant is in the business of carrying out painting and decorating
    work for the general public.

2. On April 199X the Defendant agreed to paint the full exterior of the
    Plaintiff's property at 3 Oakdale Drive, Xminster for a price of £7,000.

3. The work was carried out by the Defendant between the dates of 23 April
    and 28 April 199X inclusive, and the sum of £7,000 was paid by the
    Plaintiff to the Defendant.

4. It was an implied term of the contract made between the Plaintiff and the
    Defendant that the work would be carried out with reasonable skill and
    care.

5. In breach of that term, the work was not carried out with reasonable skill
    and care in that patches of light and dark shades were visible on the
    painted rendering of the property and during the months of July and
    August 199X the paint peeled off all the window frames at the property.

6. As a consequence the Plaintiff has suffered loss and damage.

                         PARTICULARS

    Cost of repairs to the paintwork
    and repainting where necessary   £5,500

7. The Plaintiff claims interest on any damages awarded to her as entitled
    pursuant to section 69 of the County Courts Act 1984 for such periods and
    at such rates as the Court shall think fit.

The Plaintiff therefore claims:
    i)   the sum of £5,500 under paragraph 6 above
    ii) damages
    iii) interest as previously stated
    iv) costs

Dated   199X
               Signed . . . .
                         Plaintiff
               Address . . . .

To the Chief Clerk
and to the Defendant

Fig. 10. Particulars of Claim.

68

- As regards loss for other items in a personal injury claim, such as property, incorporate a list specifying the value and entitled 'Schedule of Special Damage'.

- Your final paragraph should be indented and unnumbered. Summarise the amount and/or other remedies you claim.

- Consider including a claim for interest, similar to that in Figure 10. The interest rate is normally around 8 per cent per annum. (Check with the court office for the current rate.) Where a fixed amount is claimed such as in a debt matter, insert the interest calculated to date, and the amount per day in money terms claimed on the total until judgement or any earlier payment.

The back-sheet

Any court document will usually have attached to it a **back-sheet**. This is placed with print on the outside, to be legible when the document is face down.

The information on this is normally positioned on the right-hand side. The idea is that the document can then be folded in half lengthways, with details showing of what it is. This is traditional because barristers preferred documents folded this way, usually tied with pink tape, to be easily carried under the arm.

Figure 11 shows the format. It includes:

- the name of the court
- the case number (provided by the court office)
- the name of the case (*name of plaintiff* v *name of defendant*)
- the document's title
- the name and address of the person preparing the document.

Issuing the summons

To arrange this:

- give the court office two copies of the summons form and Particulars of Claim together with any fee
- and keep a copy of everything.

Don't be alarmed if the court clerk insists on amendments. Variations exist from court to court. Some offices are meticulous regarding a particular format. The court staff are usually helpful on procedural matters and you should take their advice on any queries.

If starting a claim in the High Court instead of the County Court

Case no. _____

IN THE XMINSTER

COUNTY COURT

BETWEEN

JOAN LANE Plaintiff

– and –

D. Z. DECORATORS
LIMITED   Defendant

PARTICULARS OF CLAIM

Joan Lane
3 Oakdale Drive
Xminster

Fig. 10. Sample back-sheet.

(though for the reasons previously given, this is unlikely) then a **writ** is issued, not a summons, with a **Statement of Claim** rather than a Particulars of Claim (though the content is similar).

THE KEY STEPS YOU MAY TAKE

What happens next depends on the circumstances of your case, but the key stages which can arise and the action which you might take are outlined here.

How long?
First a word on time-scale. Most stages are technically subject to **fourteen day time limits,** for example the defendant has fourteen days to respond to your summons.

The courts, particularly the County Court, can suffer from heavy case-loads leading to delays. Try not to get impatient if this happens. Remain polite in any enquiries made at the court office. You alienate the busy clerks there at your peril.

An admission is made
If the defendant admits your claim, he will notify the court. He may pay immediately or offer instalments. Do not turn down any reasonable proposals.

Nothing happens
If the defendant does not respond within fourteen days, you can usually apply for **judgement in default** (with costs). Calculate when the time limit is up from the note you receive from court stating the date of service.

If your claim is for a specified debt, obtain and complete form N225A. Otherwise normally form N234 applies and there will be a hearing for your damages to be assessed.

If you obtain judgement but no payment arrives, you will need to consider methods of enforcement (see Chapter 4).

Sometimes, the defendant will apply to overturn judgement to go on to defend. He will have to convince the court that there is a serious issue to be tried, and the action should continue. Even if he succeeds, he will normally have to pay any costs of judgement **being set aside**.

(One exception is if the summons was not served, for example if lost in the post. Then there is an automatic right to have the judgement set aside.)

A defence is raised

If your claim is disputed, the defendant must file a **Defence** at the court. This is a document set out in a similar format to the Particulars of Claim (*ie* same headings and structure), responding to each allegation made by you.

It may also incorporate a **Counterclaim**. This is, in effect, an action against you by the defendant, linked to the subject of your claim.

As in the small claims court, a Defence can mean that the action is transferred to a court nearer the defendant.

Right of reply

You are entitled to respond to any Defence and Counterclaim. This is done through a **Reply to Defence and Counterclaim**, in a format similar to the Particulars of Claim. You should itemise your succinct comments upon each point raised by your defendant.

Nailing down the details

If something in the defendant's Defence and/or Counterclaim is not clear, you can request **Further and Better Particulars**.

This is a formal request for something to be more specific. If, for example, the defendant makes vague allegations that you are at fault, you can ask that he clarify his argument.

A **Request for Further and Better Particulars** is the document prepared for this, usually in a layout similar to the Particulars of Claim, but it might only contain one paragraph, which comprises the questions you need to ask.

Example

'In relation to the allegation made in paragraph 4 of the Defence, the Defendant is asked to clarify the "fault" to which he refers and how he sees this as having arisen.'

Do not be taken aback if you are ever on the receiving end of such a request. They are not uncommon (particularly if the other side has a solicitor). Reply in a similar document entitled **Reply to Request for Further and Better Particulars**.

An alternative is known as an **interrogatory**. This is a question relating more to the facts of a claim. You can raise two without getting the court's permission. Specify the time allowed for an answer, usually at least twenty-eight days.

Example
'Have you received any other customer complaints in the last twelve months concerning defective lawnmowers of the same model as that involved in these proceedings?'

Affidavits

An answer to an interrogatory must be in an affidavit. This is a signed statement sworn before a solicitor. It can then usually be admitted (allowed) as evidence in court.

The solicitor may charge a small cash fee. Alternatively it can sometimes be sworn before the court staff. You repeat an oath which you will be told, with a bible in your right hand (though there are modifications for different religions, agnostics and atheists).

Affidavits may be used at other times where stated out in the court rules. They are usually headed with court details like the Particulars of Claim and commence:

'I, *name*, of *address* make oath and say as follows...'

The ending is as shown in Figure 12.

SWORN by (name)

....
                          (signature)

at (*place*)

on (*date*)

Before me

....
                          Solicitor

Fig. 12. End clause of an affidavit.

If another document, such as a letter is mentioned, a copy must be attached as an **exhibit**. This is labelled, usually with the initials of the person making the affidavit and numbered. In the affidavit, the exhibit will be referred to as follows:

'There is now produced and shown to me marked 'ABC 1' a copy of the letter dated *insert date* to which I have referred.'

Admit it!

You can use a **Notice to Admit** (again with the court heading and format like in the Particulars of Claim) to require the defendant to admit facts which he denied or has not expressly admitted. He may not then admit them – but if you incur costs in proving these at the trial (for example witness expenses) then ask that the defendant pay these.

Note that the same applies, if you are served with such a notice.

Enough pleadings

The type of document which you have been considering – like the Particulars of Claim and Defence – are known as **pleadings**.

Sooner or later, the serving of one in response to another will end. There may only be a Particulars of Claim and Defence filed anyway.

A few other procedures remain before the case gets to trial.

Getting directions

Directions are, in effect, the court's instructions on what should be done before trial. A standard type – **automatic directions** – usually apply. If not, a directions hearings or **pre-trial review** will be held to give specific directions.

Discovery

One standard direction is **discovery**. This means that each party must prepare a list of documents held (or previously held) relevant to the case.

Exceptions

Documents made essentially to assist you and not to be shown in court need not be included, for example, usually an expert's report which was not in your favour. Communications between client and solicitor also have this **privilege**.

If applicable, the list should end with:

'There are further documents in my possession but these are privileged.'

A special form (form N265), though not essential, can be obtained from a **law stationers** (specialist stockists who sell legal forms) such as Oyez Publishing Limited.

Inspection
This is when you get to see unprivileged documents held by the other side and vice versa. Usually photocopies are exchanged. If a solicitor is acting for your defendant, he may invoice you for copying charges. Object if this seems an excessive amount. If you incur copying fees, you could try charging these, or arrange instead to take your documents to the defendant/his solicitor for inspection.

Witness statements
Within ten weeks of close of pleadings, witness statements must be prepared and exchanged. Your own statement will be included.

Something known as the **hearsay rule** may soon be relaxed, but try to avoid referring to something told to you/your witnesses by a third party, such as:

'A Trading Standards officer told me he knew many problems had arisen with this product.'

This is hearsay. You really need the officer to give a statement himself.

Expert witness statements (see Chapter 4) to be used in court must also be exchanged. Two per side are allowed at the moment (or three in personal injury claims) or more with leave (consent) of court.

Setting down
As plaintiff, you must write to the court asking for a trial date. Give an estimate of how long the case will take and any dates you cannot attend. Enclose the appropriate fee (currently around £50).

Beware payments into court
Making a payment into court is a tactic your defendant may use, especially if you have rejected an offer.

You have twenty-one days to decide whether to accept the payment, usually plus costs, in settlement. If you reject it, the judge will not be told about it until after his decision. However, if he awards less or equal to that sum, you will get no costs paid – and may have to pay the defendant's costs from when the payment in was made.

Therefore think very carefully before you refuse any such payment.

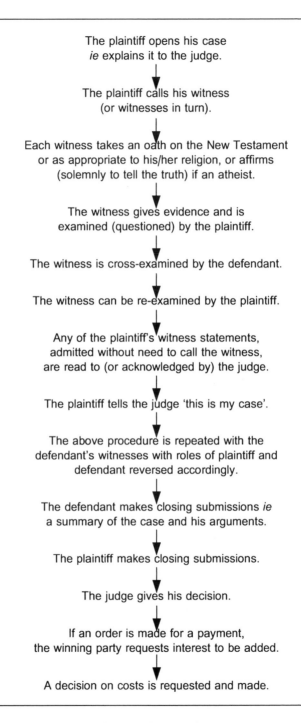

The plaintiff opens his case
ie explains it to the judge.

The plaintiff calls his witness
(or witnesses in turn).

Each witness takes an oath on the New Testament
or as appropriate to his/her religion, or affirms
(solemnly to tell the truth) if an atheist.

The witness gives evidence and is
examined (questioned) by the plaintiff.

The witness is cross-examined by the defendant.

The witness can be re-examined by the plaintiff.

Any of the plaintiff's witness statements,
admitted without need to call the witness,
are read to (or acknowledged by) the judge.

The plaintiff tells the judge 'this is my case'.

The above procedure is repeated with the
defendant's witnesses with roles of plaintiff and
defendant reversed accordingly.

The defendant makes closing submissions *ie*
a summary of the case and his arguments.

The plaintiff makes closing submissions.

The judge gives his decision.

If an order is made for a payment,
the winning party requests interest to be added.

A decision on costs is requested and made.

Fig. 13. Trial procedure.

The trial

The comments on preparation of a case in the small claims court (see Chapter 4) apply equally when it comes to a trial for a larger amount. The procedure is however, more complex.

A week before the trial, prepare an **agreed bundle** of documents. This is similar to discovery. You need to include all relevant documents, such as pleadings and other items to be referred to in court. Do not include without prejudice correspondence.

Liaise with the defendant at this stage. If he is using a solicitor, the solicitor may do the preparation. At least four copies of the bundle are normally required – so that you, the defendant, the judge and any witness have one each.

The case is heard in a traditional courtroom, usually before a **District Judge**. Where larger amounts are involved, a **Circuit Judge** may 'sit' instead. He is normally addressed as 'your Honour'.

The court will tell you of the trial date (or warn you about a week in advance of when the trial could be held). Do not be surprised if several cases are given the same time. This is because many settle at the last moment. The 'court door' factor encourages this. Other are adjourned, for example if a witness is taken ill. Because of this system, be prepared to have to wait.

The usher will tell you when to go into court and direct you where to sit. Everyone stands when the judge enters.

Figure 13 contains an outline of usual order of procedure. This may vary, depending upon the circumstances of the case.

Costs

If costs are awarded to you as a litigant in person, you can normally claim £8.24 per hour for time involved in your case, plus court fees and out-of-pocket expenses for yourself and your witnesses. (The hourly rate allowed is periodically increased, so check with the court office.)

Enforcement

If payment on the judgement is not made, consider methods of enforcement (see Chapter 4).

TAKING A SHORT CUT

Summarising the matter

Take heart that most cases do not reach a full trial. Some are disposed of by **summary judgement**.

This is good if you can persuade the court to grant it (often at the pre-trial review stage). Apply for it on the standard form obtainable from the court office, accompanied by an affidavit stating the circumstances and that you believe that there is no proper defence to your claim. The defendant may submit his own affidavit in response.

Summary judgement is appropriate where the defence is weak (sometimes just a ploy to delay payment).

Don't forget to ask for costs. (It is a good idea to ask for them in any court application. If nothing else, you may at least recover court fees.)

Settling out of court

So many cases settle out of court that you should not be surprised if the defendant starts without prejudice negotiations (see Chapter 4).

CASE STUDIES

These follow on from the situation in the Particulars of Claim in Figure 10. Each represents a possible development in Joan Lane's action.

Joan goes for summary judgement

When Joan receives a copy of the Defence, she suspects that this is just a delaying tactic, perhaps because the company has cash-flow problems. The Defence is, on the face of it, very weak and makes vague references to freak weather conditions being responsible for damage to the paintwork. It also suggests that Joan contributed to the damage by using an unsuitable cleaning product on the window frames.

Joan contacts the court for the appropriate application form for summary judgement. She completes and files this at court, with an affidavit in support.

The District Judge considers the matter. It is touch and go but he gives D. Z. Decorators Ltd the benefit of the doubt. Nevertheless, he feels that the defence is 'shadowy'. To help Joan, he gives only **conditional leave to defend**. This means that judgement will be given unless the defendant pays into court the amount claimed. Joan then knows that if she is successful, the money will be there to pay her.

Joan settles out of court

Suppose, instead, Joan requires Further and Better Particulars of the Defence. The reply indicates that the Defence may be stronger than first appeared.

Joan then receives a 'without prejudice' letter from the defendant's solicitor offering £4,000. Joan rejects this. The solicitor makes a payment into court of this amount.

Joan now feels under pressure. If she does not 'beat' the payment-in at the trial, she will have to pay the defendant's legal costs from this time onwards. She decides to take the bird in the hand and accepts the payment.

At the court door

Suppose instead the action continues. Joan finds, however, that the defendant's solicitor is dragging his heels in completing the procedure.

She writes to him about this. She receives a telephone call in response. The solicitor insinuates that she is naïve to expect the technical time limits to be met. She takes no notice. She mentions that she is considering applying for an **unless order** to state that unless the defendant carries out the required action by a set date then the defendant will be debarred from proceeding at all.

The outstanding matter is dealt with by the solicitor within seven days. Nevertheless, he tries a new tactic and applies for **security for costs**. This is an order than Joan pay an amount into court to cover the defendant's costs if she loses. It is not granted because Joan's case is not tenuous, nor is she impecunious or living abroad, and no other reason is found to justify it.

The case is listed for trial. The parties attend on the date set. In the courtroom corridor, Joan is approached by the solicitor with an offer of £4,500. Joan decides that this is preferable to the risk of losing in court, but stipulates that her court fees must also be paid, plus an amount to cover her time and out-of-pocket expenses.

The court is told of the arrangement agreed and this is made into a consent order. This will help ensure Joan gets prompt payment or, failing this, she can take enforcement procedure straight away.

SUMMARY

- Decide whether to instruct a solicitor.

- Make sure you send a letter before action.

- If this is unproductive, consider proceedings.

- Bear in mind the cost risk.

- If you proceed, choose the appropriate court (usually the County Court).

- Prepare a Particulars of Claim and issue a summons.

- If no Defence is received, apply for judgement in default with costs.

- If appropriate, apply for summary judgement with costs.

- Follow through the procedures as appropriate to your case – such as pleadings, directions, discovery, inspections, exchange of witness statements and setting down.

- Always consider any reasonable offer made to you. If you accept, have the agreement recorded in writing or embodied in a consent order.

- Be as methodical as possible at the trial. Ask for costs if you win.

DISCUSSION POINTS

1. In which court do you think that the following might find themselves?

    (a) Pauline Jones of Colchester who had new kitchen units fitted by XY Kitchens Ltd, but has encountered endless quality problems. Full repair will cost £3,500.

    (b) Ronald Grainger who purchased a new kettle for £35. Due to a fault, it exploded causing him severe personal injuries estimated at £60,000 and property damage of £2,000.

2. Draft a Particulars of Claim based on Pauline Jones's situation at (a) above.

3. What are the important points to remember when accepting any offer?

6
Using a Solicitor

ASSESSING THE COST

Why bother with a solicitor?

There are good reasons for involving a solicitor in a claim, particularly one over the small claims court £3,000 limit. Examples are:

- you should gain a better idea of the strength of your case

- you do not have to trek by yourself through the current maze of court procedure

- documents are drafted for you

- the solicitor's expertise may make the difference between win and lose

- a solicitor has resources at hand, such as case reports, textbooks, fax, secretarial and sometimes research assistants, computer facilities and perhaps access to the Internet.

Information may be available to a solicitor which you would find difficult to access. The Association of Personal Injury Lawyers, for example, has a Product Defect Register on claims made about 'dud' products.

A solicitor can sometimes give you prudent advice not to proceed, and avoid your wasting time and expense, or if you do proceed, he can help make sure it is successful. Recent figures suggest a 90 per cent failure rate by litigants in person in seeking leave to appeal, when required.

Nevertheless fear of the **cost** all this could entail can be off-putting.

How is the cost worked out?

Bear in mind that in **contentious** (litigation/court) matters, a solicitor's bill is based above all on time taken. With **non-contentious** matters (like conveyancing on a house purchase) a figure, based partly on the value involved, is usually agreed in advance.

It is more difficult for a solicitor to predict cost when he/she cannot guarantee the outcome. Will it be possible to get summary judgement or to settle, or will the action proceed all the way to trial?

A solicitor essentially bills for his **time**, based upon a 'charge-out rate'. This can vary from firm to firm, and depends upon the seniority of the solicitor. He also includes disbursements (expenses like court fees) and may charge for **care and conduct**. The more complex the case, the larger this is.

Ask in advance for some estimate of the likely cost – particularly the hourly rate – before you given **instructions** (*ie* ask the solicitor to represent you).

New clients should be given a 'client care letter', generally detailing costs, a rough estimate of the length of time the case will take and the person to complain to at the firm, if ever necessary.

What's the brief?
It may later prove necessary to employ a **barrister** (referred to as **Counsel**) to appear in court or to give an opinion on your case. At present, the public can normally only approach a barrister through contact (or **brief**) by a solicitor. (There are new proposals for referrals through Citizens Advice Bureaux for claims under £10,000). The most senior and expensive barrister is a **Queen's Counsel** (or 'silk'). Barristers operate from offices known as **chambers**.

The need for both a solicitor and barrister has decreased because some solicitors are now allowed to **appear** (present a case) in the High Court, as well as County Court. They are known as **solicitor-advocates**. The first of this new breed (ironically an ex-barrister) made his High Court début in February 1994. They appear in many cases, from contract to VAT. They must pass a tough (and expensive) test first, which has prevented vast expansion in this field.

Paying money up front
Often your solicitor will ask for money 'on account of costs' to cover court fees and initial preparation, plus any barrister's fees before sending out a brief.

Making the decision
Instructing a solicitor needs careful consideration. Even if you win and are awarded costs, there may be a shortfall between what the defendant has to pay and your solicitor's bill. This is because assessment of costs for the defendant may be on a different basis to that charged to you.

You have to pay the difference.

Costs are always at the court's discretion, so you could win and not receive any (though this is unusual). If the court feels that you (or your solicitor) implemented some procedure unnecessarily, then it may stipulate no costs be awarded for this particular aspect.

There is the possibility of legal aid or a 'no win, no fee' arrangement (see page 86). You may have some legal expenses insurance (a small but growing market in the UK). Most major insurers offer it, together with organisations like the AA.

OBTAINING PRELIMINARY ADVICE

It is useful to obtain an authoritative opinion as to whether you have a case and it is worth incurring a small sum for this, rather than risking large court costs on a no-hoper. If you receive social security benefits, you may obtain free advice under the **green form scheme** (see page 84).

Getting initial feedback on your case

You could contact a consumer body, like a **Citizens Advice Bureau** (see Chapter 7).

Some solicitors operate a **fixed fee interview scheme**, whereby you pay around £10 for a half-hour consultation upon the merits of your case. Fewer firms have offered this since the recession, but it is worth enquiring locally. Some advertise a free first interview, often aimed at a particular area of law, such as family problems.

You may find that you are interviewed by a trainee or a **legal executive**. There is no reason they cannot give you good preliminary advice and it may cost less than for an experienced solicitor.

Choosing a firm of solicitors

Recommendation is important. If none of your friends can help, study advertisements carefully. Solicitors are allowed to advertise more extensively and can incorporate more 'sales puff' than before. Consider telephoning the receptionist for details of how long the firm has been established and who's who there. Many have a brochure which you can ask to be sent to you.

You could approach a firm you have dealt with before, such as on your house sale (provided they gave you a good service). The person who acted for you previously may not deal with matters like your complaint, but will refer you to a colleague who does. Often if you are an established client, a firm will not bill you for a short discussion, as a gesture of goodwill.

Recent developments

Lawyers have been urged to carry out more **pro bono** work (for the good of the public *ie* without charge). Some impetus for this comes from a Judges Council plan. This focuses upon the Royal Courts of Justice in London and links to an expanded role for the Citizens Advice Bureau.

One MP has recently called for a national legal service (echoing some ideas around in the 1970s).

One interesting – though perhaps still very experimental – development has been the **Law Shop**. A Bristol firm provided a kind of half-way house between instructing a solicitor and acting for yourself. At modest cost you can:

- buy a particular legal form, kit or book to help with your case

- pay an admission charge (about £6 per visit) to use facilities including advice from a solicitor on duty (ten minutes free, with a small charge for more time).

APPLYING FOR LEGAL AID

What is legal aid?

Legal aid is not, and has never been, widely accessible like the National Health Service. Recent cut-backs have meant that many people are no longer financially eligible. This has tended to stress the old cliché that 'only the very rich or the very poor can afford to go to law'.

If you are eligible, it can give you a safeguard against costs. Legal aid will cover your solicitor's/barrister's fees and your court fees. If you lose, the court will rarely order you to pay the other side's costs. (A few, such as ex-Master of the Rolls, Lord Denning, have suggested this be changed, and recent plans may modify the position.)

When can you get legal aid?

Legal aid is available for most proceedings, such as divorce, repossession, contract and tort. There are exceptions, like libel/slander and most consumer claims within the small claims court limit (see Chapter 4).

A legal aid certificate may be limited to certain steps, or your solicitor may need authorisation to go beyond a certain level of costs.

Green form

You can sometimes receive a type of legal aid known as **legal advice and assistance** through completing a certain green form. This covers preliminary consultation and steps, like sending a solicitor's letter. Nowadays, this is mainly available to those on benefit.

Full legal aid
This covers court proceedings. Your solicitor can supply the application forms, which are sent to the Legal Aid Office for your area.

There are two tests which you must pass:

- merit – your case must have a reasonable prospect of success
- means – you must be within the financial limits.

Although the current budget for civil legal aid is £675 million, you may feel that the means test is fairly mean. Limits change every April (usually to become narrower). How much you are allowed to earn and the capital you can have, but still qualify for legal aid, depends upon whether you have children and/or a partner to support. Other factors, like whether your claim is for personal injuries can affect this. There are special rules for pensioners. Equity in a house can be taken into account over a certain amount.

In broad terms, for 1996/7:

- if you receive state benefits you automatically qualify

- if you have income between £2,498 and £7,403 and/or savings over £3,000, you will probably have to pay a **contribution**

- over a certain income or level of capital depending on your circumstances, you will receive no legal aid.

You are told about any contribution you must pay. The rest is covered by the Legal Aid Fund.

The statutory charge
If the defendant ends up paying your costs, these go to the Legal Aid Office. Otherwise the price of your legal aid can be deducted from your compensation. This is because, under statute, a charge is placed upon any property or money you recover. In matrimonial cases, it can have the effect that the party who gets the house, takes it subject to this charge, which bears interest.

How do you get legal aid?
Most applications are through a solicitor. (A few charge for preparing

the forms.) You can tell if a firm takes legal aid work if it displays the appropriate sign in its window, showing two 'stick' people sitting opposite each other at a desk.

Recently, more legal aid work has been done by **franchised** firms (those with a special arrangement with the Legal Aid Board). Recent plans indicate they will be the main legal aid solicitors.

Fund-holding (similar to that in the NHS) and standard fees (similar to America's health service) may be introduced into legal aid. There may soon be a minimum contribution or fee payable by all who receive legal aid.

OPTING FOR 'NO WIN, NO FEE'

A 'No win, no fee' arrangement with a lawyer means that if you don't win, you don't pay him/her.

It is known as a **conditional fee** basis. It was outlawed here and contrary to the rules of the Law Society (which governs solicitors) partly because of fear that it would encourage unprofessional behaviour like 'ambulance chasing' by solicitors.

It is now allowed, provided it is within a set statutory framework. The main time when it is likely to apply is if you do not qualify for legal aid but have a personal injury claim, or for medical negligence or insolvency cases. Recent plans may extend it to most cases.

How much will it cost if you win?

Because they risk not being paid if you lose, solicitors/barristers will probably charge more than usual if you win. How much depends upon the agreement you reach, but the Law Society proposes a ceiling of 25 per cent above formal fees.

Costs can be taken from any damages awarded, but may be off-set (at least in part) by any costs which the defendant has to pay.

What if you lose?

A conditional fee agreement does not take away the risk of your being ordered by the court to pay the other side's costs (see also Chapters 4 and 5). You may also remain liable for other expenses, like witness and court fees.

Insurance against the risk is becoming available.

Example
A special policy called *Accident Line Protect* has been launched by the Law Society. At the time of writing, for a premium of £85, you can be

covered for £100,000 of your opponent's legal fees. Your expert witness fees and other disbursements will also be covered. Your own barristers' fees are not included because it is assumed they will agree to 'no win, no fee' like solicitors. There are special provisions regarding payments into court (see Chapter 5) – some of which are optional – and should be discussed thoroughly with your solicitor.

A **contingency** fee agreement, as in America where a lawyer receives a percentage of any compensation, is generally unenforceable here, because it is seen as against public policy. A solicitor who enters such an agreement can suffer serious consequences.

CASE STUDIES

Pam was involved in an accident when a delivery van knocked her from her bicycle. She has suffered personal injuries including a broken wrist. The driver, his employers and their insurers have denied liability. She has no legal insurance, but wishes to consult a solicitor. The courses she might take are outlined below.

Pam makes a choice

Pam obtains a recommendation from a friend. She also telephones the firm who dealt with her house purchase.

One solicitor is confident about her chances of success, but vague on his own costs. He will not disclose his hourly rate or give any estimate, but reassures her that the outcome will be that the driver's insurance will pay for everything. Nevertheless, he requires an initial sum from her on account of costs.

The other solicitor stresses the difficulty of giving an accurate estimate but states an hourly rate and the amount of likely disbursements. He offers a free interview, at which to take details. From this, he feels he should be able to assess the strength of her case and whether she is eligible for legal aid. Pam makes an appointment with him.

Making a contribution

At the interview, the solicitor feels that Pam's case is good. He discusses legal aid.

As she is in part-time employment on a modest salary, Pam does not qualify for green form advice, but she is likely to obtain legal aid to bring proceedings. The solicitor explains the statutory charge, and assists her in completing the necessary forms.

The Legal Aid Office are satisfied that Pam has a case. After her means have been assessed, she is offered legal aid, subject to paying a contribution, which can be made by monthly instalments.

On condition

Perhaps if Pam had not qualified for legal aid, she might have considered a 'no win, no fee' agreement. It should be possible for an arrangement to be made within the permitted statutory framework, supported by suitable insurance. This will probably be *Accident Line*, if her solicitor is a member of the Law Society's Personal Injury Panel.

She should discuss all the agreement and insurance in detail with the solicitor, paying particular attention to probabilities, like a payment into court.

SUMMARY

- Approach recommended solicitors for cost estimates.

- Obtain preliminary advice, if possible under the green form scheme, or on a fixed fee/free initial interview basis.

- Ascertain whether you may qualify for legal aid.

- If so, bear in mind the statutory charge.

- Consider whether a 'no win, no fee' agreement may suit your circumstances.

DISCUSSION POINTS

1. What criteria would you use to choose a solicitor to represent you in any claim?

2. List the questions you might ask to ascertain if the solicitor meets your criteria.

3. What important points would you raise concerning the costs of any action?

7
Taking the Alternatives

IS THERE AN ALTERNATIVE?

Today there seems to be an alternative to everything available, from medicine to comedy. **Alternative Dispute Resolution** (ADR) is the new buzzword for other ways of resolving a dispute, as an alternative to court proceedings.

Many of these can help you achieve a quick, economic solution to problems.

WHAT ARE THE OPTIONS?

Some alternatives, like arbitration, mediation and conciliation, are methods of reaching a solution which are practised by certain bodies. Certain firms now specialise in these areas. Others, like Ombudsmen, are persons specially appointed to deal with certain types of dispute (see Chapters 8 and 9). There are also authorities, like the Advertising Standards Authority, to whom you can complain on certain matters, and organisations, like Citizens Advice Bureaux, who may be able to give you general assistance.

CHOOSING THE RIGHT ONE

To help you select an appropriate option, the main alternatives are summarised below.

Arbitration
What is it?
Note that this arbitration is not the same as arbitration in the small claims court (see Chapter 4). Here it broadly means the determination of a dispute by a person appointed by agreement between the parties involved.

You might find that a small print condition in a contract stipulates that any complaint you have must be referred to arbitration. Such a condition is unlikely to be binding on you **as a consumer**. There can be exceptions, such as if you consent to arbitration **after** the dispute has arisen or sometimes if a contract of insurance is involved.

What happens?
A person is nominated as arbitrator and fixes a time for his/her hearing of the dispute.

You (and your opponent) are usually allowed to present your case and call witnesses. The arbitrator takes account of the law and the points put forward. He/she makes a decision (giving reasons) and says which party is to pay any expenses.

What then?
Usually the parties abide by the arbitrator's decision. The courts can usually only change the decision through **judicial review** in the High Court and in limited circumstances, such as if the arbitrator made an error of law.

Mediation and conciliation
Mediation generally involves a go-between who is **proactive**, putting forward possible solutions. Conciliation is aimed at getting the parties to meet on middle-ground. The two terms are becoming more inter-changeable.

About 80 per cent of ADR processes involve mediation/conciliation. America, Canada, Australia and Hong Kong are just a few countries to develop their own forms. Here, the CBI is promoting such methods.

The basis is usually that an independent person introduces a structure whereby you and your opponent reach a workable solution. In the wise old words of Francis Bacon:

'It is generally better to deal by speech than by letter; and by mediation of a third party than by a man's self.'

Mediation and conciliation can be speedy and cheap compared with court action, and organised anywhere, though preferably on neutral ground. These methods are not, however, a good idea for any issue you feel should attract publicity, as confidentiality is often one of the rules laid down.

Recently some charitable organisations have set up mediation and conciliation services to help in such areas as family matters and one – Mediation UK – specialises in neighbour disputes. It is unlikely that ADR here will develop to the extremes it has in America (for example, 'rent-a-judge' arrangements as in a case involving Clint Eastwood). Nevertheless these methods are being incorporated into more and more ordinary dealings. Furthermore, many ombudsmen (see Chapters 8 and 9) have the power to conciliate as well as adjudicate (decide) in disputes. A British Association of Lawyer Mediators now exists.

Trade associations

If your complaint is against a business which is a member of a trade association (usually indicated on notepaper or a sign) the association may offer to arbitrate in a dispute. This is normally free of charge, but check the terms of the arbitration. You may find that the decision is binding upon you if you agree to use arbitration.

The Office of Fair Trading (OFT)

This may become involved in certain issues (see Chapters 2 and 10). If you think these issues overlap with your particular case, it may be worth contacting the OFT.

Example
A consumer recently tipped off the OFT regarding concern over local pricing practices for residential conveyancing. The OFT investigated whether anti-competitive practices existed, with a view to stamping out any minimum price agreement.

Trading Standards Departments

Local Trading Standards officers can also help you in certain matters (see Chapter 10).

Environmental Health Departments

These can help with complaints about, for example, mouldy food or food poisoning connected with a restaurant, public house or shop. They are listed in the phone book with other local authority services.

The Data Protection Registrar

You have rights under the **Data Protection Act 1984**. The Data Protection Registrar can be instrumental in bringing prosecutions and imposing penalties for misuse of personal data. He (or she as at present) can serve

- **an enforcement notice** requiring compliance with the regulations
- **a de-registration notice**, which can be disastrous to some businesses.

The Advertising Standards Authority

This can investigate complaints free of charge about advertisements and promotions in non-broadcast media. Submit your complaint in writing with a copy of the advertisement(s) concerned. Your identity will not be revealed to the advertiser.

Matters which amount to breach of a code of practice are given priority. The first principle of the Advertising Code is that:

All advertisements should be legal, decent, honest and truthful.

Industry regulators

There are also certain bodies who can help with particular types of complaint. Within the privatised industries, for example, you can contact OFWAT (water services), OFFER (electricity), OFTEL (telecommunications) and OFGAS or the Gas Consumer Council (gas services), depending upon your problem. (Addresses of these and other organisations are at the back of this book.)

The National Consumer Council (NCC)

'We speak up for the consumers of goods and services of all kinds,' says the NCC which campaigns on behalf of consumers. It does not deal directly with individual queries, but takes up wide-scale issues.

The Consumers Association

Membership can bring many benefits. The Association has full-time qualified staff who can assist in most types of consumer matters.

Citizens Advice Bureaux (CAB)

CABs can give you free advice. Sometimes they may write on your behalf to the other side or help you present your case to, say, an ombudsman.

Mainly they are manned by volunteers with basic legal training. Often they arrange for local solicitors to hold free advice sessions one evening per week.

Law Centres

These offer a similar service but often have full-time legally qualified staff. They can represent you in most matters.

Law Centres have suffered from funding cut-backs. There may, however, be one in your locality (check *Yellow Pages*). Wandsworth, for example, survived funding loss partly due to Law Society help. Several reputable solicitors firms staff a 'surgery' once a week. Lottery money may open a mobile centre in Carlisle.

Legal Advice Centres

A few of these are run at local level, often as charities, for example Fulham Legal Advice Centre. Many staff are volunteers, including solicitors and barristers who donate time for evening consultations.

CASE STUDIES

Litigate or arbitrate?

Clare and Tim are first-time buyers of a Victorian terrace house. A condition of their mortgage offer is that they carry out damp-proofing and timber works. The work is undertaken by Stop-the-Rot Ltd who issue a thirty-year guarantee.

Two years later, Clare notices fresh sawdust on the wooden staircase. They call the company back. A dispute arises over whether the re-infestation of woodworm is due to defective timber treatment or has come from an untreated hall-stand which Clare purchased recently from an antiques shop.

The company is a member of an association of wood preservers and damp-proofers. Clare and Tim consider court action but feel that they cannot afford this. They agree instead to refer the matter to arbitration as provided by the association. They pay for an opinion by another specialist firm to support their allegations. The arbitrator decides in their favour and this expense is awarded to them. The company must also make good the defective work.

Bureau action

Jim and Patricia are married with two young children. They have come through a bad patch financially, following Jim's redundancy. Jim now has a new job and his first monthly salary is due to be paid via the BACS system into their building society account. In anticipation, they have committed themselves to several purchases. Furthermore, as they are not now receiving benefit, it is vital to their everyday finances that the money is available to them on the anticipated date.

Unfortunately when that day arrives, Patricia is told by the society that she cannot withdraw from the account because it is overdrawn.

Patricia visits her local Citizens Advice Bureau. An advice worker telephones Jim's employers' accounts department and the building society. It is established that the money has been sent but, due to the account number being wrongly quoted, it has been placed in a suspense account at the society.

The advice worker informs the branch manager that unless the situation is immediately rectified, the bureau will assist Patricia with a claim to the Building Societies Ombudsman.

When Patricia returns to the branch, the account has been credited and she makes a withdrawal. The branch manager explains that an *ex gratia* payment of £20 has been added for inconvenience.

Data fairness

Sally receives a call asking if she will spare a few minutes to assist with market research related to home furnishings. Sally answers certain questions.

A few weeks later, Sally receives an inordinate amount of junk mail and cold-calling from firms who fit kitchens. She recalls that the 'research survey' placed emphasis upon kitchen fitments and suspects a link.

If Sally is correct, she could consider complaining to the Data Protection Registrar over a possible breach of the Data Protection Act and principles. The provisions emphasise that data should be obtained fairly and lawfully. Here it seems that 'market research' could possibly have been a bogus excuse to obtain details about her to supply to companies as a potential customer. If so, she ought to have been informed when she decided to give the information, as stressed by a recent Data Protection Tribunal decision.

SUMMARY

- Before you sue, consider the alternatives.

- With new initiatives towards ADR, various types of mediation and arbitration are becoming available.

- These alternatives can have the advantages of speed and economy over traditional court action.

- Bodies like the Advertising Standards Authority can also help with certain complaints.

- Other organisations like CABs can give you general assistance.

DISCUSSION POINTS

Consider again the case studies in Chapters 4 and 5.

1. Which of these situations might have been suitable for ADR?

2. Which particular alternatives could have been appropriate?

3. What might have been the advantages in each case of using an alternative to court action?

8
Complaining to Financial
Services Ombudsmen

WHAT IS AN OMBUDSMAN?

Scandinavia first developed the concept of an ombudsman. The name originally meant 'legal representative', but came to stand for a person who decides the outcome of a dispute. An ombudsman is therefore similar to a judge but outside the court system.

One difference is that an ombudsman tends to be **inquisitorial**, rather than **adversarial**. Despite the connotations of old ideas of the Spanish Inquisition, this really just means that an ombudsman tends to look at a case as a whole. He can have a more hands-on approach to directing how it is presented. He tends to concentrate upon documentary evidence. Court judges on the other hand, mainly listen to arguments put by the different sides as adversaries and then decide which has convinced them.

WHO ARE THE FS (FINANCIAL SERVICES) OMBUDSMEN?

There are now ombudsmen schemes in many countries, from Australia to South America. In the UK, they began in the public sector (covering parliamentary and local government activities) and are now used in the private sector, particularly financial services.

Ombudsmen schemes have increased in the eighties and nineties. For the financial institutions, they can mean less 'washing dirty linen in public'. For the individual, they can offer a quick alternative to court – and free of charge.

Figure 14 is a diagram of the main FS Ombudsmen and indicates the broad category of complaint each may sometimes consider.

The names of the particular ombudsmen are not stated, because the individuals change from time to time. At the time of writing, several are due to retire with new appointments to be announced in the near future.

Ombudsmen are usually referred to in the masculine form for convenience. Whilst most happen to be men, there is nothing to preclude an 'ombudswoman' – though she is usually referred to as an

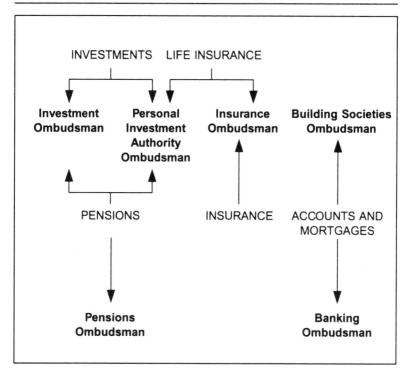

Fig. 14. The main FS ombudsmen.

ombudsman anyway. An example is the late Jane Woodhead, who acted as joint Building Societies Ombudsman for several years.

WHAT CASES CAN THEY HANDLE?

The six main FS Ombudsmen in Figure 14 have their particular area or **jurisdiction**. Below is a summary of the types of complaint each is likely to handle. There can be some overlap, as you will see.

The Insurance Ombudsman

He was the first financial services ombudsman. He investigates complaints concerning general insurance such as household or motor insurance (except those relating to a third party's insurer). Life policies are another of his areas, but recently the Personal Investment Authority (PIA) Ombudsman has taken over most such cases. Occasionally the Insurance Ombudsman deals with personal pensions, but these usually go to the PIA or Pensions Ombudsmen.

If insurers are not a member of the Insurance Ombudsman Bureau, they may belong to the **Arbitration Service of the Chartered Institute of Arbitrators**, which may be able to help you instead.

The Banking Ombudsman

His role is based upon a voluntary scheme entered by the major banks. He can help you if you have a complaint concerning a bank account, or a matter like an automatic teller machine (ATM or 'hole-in-the-wall machine), credit card, mortgage or other loan connected with a bank. Occasionally he may handle an insurance matter, depending on your bank's involvement in this.

The Building Societies Ombudsman (BS Ombudsman)

His scheme was set up under the Building Societies Act 1986 – though the blueprint for this was the Banking Ombudsman scheme. The two ombudsmen therefore deal with similar matters, but the BS Ombudsman helps where you have a problem with a building society. He looks at matters relating to investment accounts, ATMs, mortgages and other loans. Some complaints over credit cards can be considered under a special arrangement. Some insurance matters can be investigated depending on the involvement of any building society.

> **When building societies convert to plc status, they become banks. The timing of both the conversion and when the substance of your complaint arose, may determine whether you refer to the BS Ombudsman or the Banking Ombudsman.**

The Investment Ombudsman

This ombudsman's jurisdiction is complex, particularly since the growth of the PIA. This is because historically there has been a maze of regulatory bodies, such as LAUTRO, FIMBRA and IMRO. The ombudsman has jurisdiction over companies affiliated to IMRO (Investment Manager Regulatory Organisation). The company stationery should reveal if this is the case, or a direct enquiry with the organisation.

The Investment Ombudsman deals with complaints such as advice leading up to the sale of an endowment policy, the purchase and sale of shares, and unit trusts. However, if the company belongs to the PIA, then his ambit is limited and you may find an approach to the PIA Ombudsman is more appropriate.

The Pensions Ombudsman

He deals mainly with occupational pension schemes, and sometimes investigates alleged maladminstration (see page 104) together with some matters regarding personal pensions.

His jurisdiction has been affected by the PIA Ombudsman, who takes any complaints which involve the selling/marketing of personal pension schemes. Under a special agreement, the Insurance Ombudsman may step in instead to investigate complains over the management of some personal pension schemes.

The Personal Investment Authority Ombudsman (The PIA Ombudsman)

He is the latest of the main FS Ombudsmen. The office was set up in 1994 by Stephen Edell (formerly BS Ombudsman). It was no easy task due to the complexities of jurisdiction and 'who deals with what'.

The role of the PIA Ombudsman is very important and a move towards having an adjudicator for retail financial services as a whole. He can investigate all aspects of investment business, such as unit trusts and PEPS carried out by PIA members. Many providers of financial services, like building societies, are members and the organisation's stationery may state this. If not, enquire direct with the organisation or at the PIA or PIA Ombudsman's office.

As regards personal pensions and life assurance, the PIA Ombudsman can investigate complaints concerning sales/marketing, plus other matters like maladministration (see page 104) if the particular company has agreed that he may do so.

One of the matters which the PIA Ombudsman takes into account is observance of the Financial Services Act 1986, particularly the requirement for 'best advice' to be given.

RECOGNISING YOUR TYPE OF COMPLAINT

Before you select an ombudsman to approach, be clear on what your complaint is. To help in this:

• Write down the main facts.

• List the ways in which you feel that a particular organisation was to blame.

• Decide which of these are the most serious by asking yourself what is **the essence** of your complaint.

Example

Suppose your building society failed to carry out your express instructions for it to set up adequate endowment cover to repay your mortgage at the end of the mortgage term. Errors in the written statements which you have received have masked this problem for some time. When you recently queried the matter, you received no reply to your letters and a member of staff was rude to you on the telephone.

You write a summary of the relevant facts and list your allegations against the society. It is clear that the essence of your complaint is that the society failed to set up adequate endowment cover. The errors in the statements were minor inefficiencies which confounded and added to this. The mis-handling of your queries is another ancillary matter, which should be brought to the ombudsman's attention, but is not the main thrust of your case.

WHICH OMBUDSMAN TO CHOOSE?

- Once you have identified the essence of your complaint, look at the summaries given earlier of the different ombudsmen.

- Decide which best fits your complaint.

- There may be more than one ombudsman who can potentially investigate your complaint.

- If only one ombudsman is appropriate, contact his office. You may have to send full details in writing.

- If more than one may be appropriate, choose one. Write or telephone and ask to speak to a complaints officer or similar employee. He/she will help you decide which ombudsman would be best for your complaint. You may have to send full details in writing.

- If you have a choice between the PIA Ombudsman and another, it may be best to contact the PIA Ombudsman's office first. They will steer you in the right direction.

Example

Following through from the example previously given, the essence of your complaint has been identified as the failure by a building society to set up the endowment as per your instructions. Therefore, although it involves a life policy with an insurance company, the complaint is essentially against the society for its incompetence. The society may be a member of the PIA but you are not querying an investment aspect of the endowment. Therefore the BS Ombudsman is likely to be the best one to approach.

DEALING WITH OVERLAPPING CLAIMS

A complaint can be dealt with by more than one ombudsman. Some complaints involve two organisations. An example might be if a building society arranged in error the wrong insurance for you and the insurance company also failed to note details which you supplied to it. In such cases, it is not unknown for two ombudsmen to deal with the complaint together in tandem. This ensures that you are not compensated for the same loss twice (contrary to fundamental legal principles) and allocates the responsibility properly between any parties at fault.

If you face a choice between ombudsmen, the following may help:

* Discuss the situation with the respective complaints sections (sometimes known as 'New Complaints Departments') at the ombudsmen's offices. Some may insist that you write with details.

* Note that some ombudsmen have greater powers than others. The PIA Ombudsman can only usually award a maximum of up to £50,000 (though this may change). Others like the Insurance Ombudsman and the BS Ombudsman can award up to £100,000.

* Depending upon workloads from time to time, one office may be able to progress your complaint more quickly than another. At the time of writing, the insurance ombudsman's office (through no fault of its own) can take longer than, for example, the BS Ombudsman's office (the present ombudsman, Brian Murphy, having made much progress to speed up the process).

PURSUING YOUR CASE

Each ombudsman scheme varies in exact procedure. Usually you must first complain to the organisation concerned. With the Insurance Ombudsman, you need to go through the Occupational Pensions Advisory Service; with the Investment Ombudsman, you go through IMRO.

Most ombudsmen are reluctant to investigate before a **deadlock** situation is reached. Sometimes it is stated that you must **exhaust the**

internal complaints procedure (ICP) of the organisation concerned.

This can be frustrating, particularly if your complaint relates to members of staff, who may be involved in the ICP. The reasoning behind the deadlock requirement is that the organisation may sort out any misunderstanding and/or find a compromise acceptable to you.

You may find that, once you indicate an intention to go to an ombudsman, an offer is made. Most organisations seek to avoid the administration time and any expense which the procedure may entail for them.

The organisation should provide you with details of its ICP and ombudsman scheme on request. Most banks and building societies have relevant leaflets.

What do I do next?
Contact the ombudsman's office and deal with an officer who handles new complaints. Some discuss cases over the telephone, others need you to write in.

Make early contact. Sometimes there are time limits. Some ombudsmen rule out complaints six months after deadlock. The BS Ombudsman has a discretion not to investigate if you are guilty of undue delay. Notifying his office of the substance of your complaint can help stop the clock running against you.

Some ombudsmen's offices send you their particular type of **complaints form**. You may first have to produce a deadlock letter from the organisation you claim against, confirming its ICP is exhausted.

COMPLETING A COMPLAINTS FORM

Many complainants do not do justice to themselves at this stage. They allow emotional involvement and often well-justified anger, to prevent their clearly stating the position.

Whilst the exact details required vary from ombudsman to ombudsman, the following suggestions may help you avoid this danger when you set out your complaint:

- Firstly fill in any basic details requested, such as your name, address and details of the organisation concerned.

- **Summarise the relevant facts** before you get involved in the issues.

- Do not make the mistake of thinking of the ombudsman as some naïve 'ivory tower' individual, who can be won over by mere rhetoric.

- Follow the guidelines given earlier under 'Recognising your type of complaint.' **State clearly the main aspect of your complaint**.

- You can refer to earlier correspondence instead provided this fully encapsulates your complaint.

- Refer to the evidence (for example, letters, agreements, receipts) which support your allegations made by you. Enclose copies.

- Enclose brief signed statements from any witnesses who support your allegations/version of events.

- Mention subsidiary aspects, such as delay in the ICP. Provide copy correspondence or other evidence backing this up.

- State the amount you are claiming and how this is calculated, enclosing copies of any quotations, invoices and/or receipts.

- State any other steps you wish the ombudsmen to direct, for example, 'order rectification of entries on my account'.

- Enclose copies of relevant correspondence and documentation in general.

How much can I claim?

This depends upon the ombudsman scheme involved. For many the limit is £100,000 – though most ombudsmen's awards are for considerably less. Claim for any loss you feel you have suffered, plus expenses, including letters and telephone calls.

Some make awards for time spent on the complaint based upon the court's rate for a litigant in person (currently around £8.25 per hour). Claim also for any solicitors' or other professional help in your complaint. There is no guarantee that the ombudsman will award this. He is unlikely to do so unless there was justifiable need to consult them, and their charges are reasonable.

Many ombudsmen can award for **inconvenience** (unlike the usual situation in court, which can be another good reason for choosing an ombudsman alternative). Inconvenience covers distress, disappointment and general hassle suffered in the matter.

WHAT HAPPENS NEXT?

This depends on the particular ombudsman's office. In general your complaint is considered by a legally-qualified member of staff (often a barrister or solicitor). They may be referred to as a Legal Officer or Case Officer.

If preliminary points occur to that person, he/she may contact you. Examples could be:

- **Delay**. You may have to clarify dates or explain delay. Perhaps you were seriously ill, or unaware that the ombudsman existed.

- **Jurisdiction**. You may be asking for something which the ombudsman cannot give, or you may need to approach another ombudsman.

- **Conciliation**. An offer may be made which you may be wise to accept.

Otherwise, a copy of your complaints form will usually be sent to the organisation for its comments (or **representations**) and replies to specific enquiries. If the organisation finds it difficult to answer, an offer may suddenly materialise.

Once representations are received, the case is usually considered by the ombudsman. Many schemes (such as that of the BS Ombudsman) require him to give an indication or **preliminary conclusion** of his views. With the Banking Ombudsman, you may receive an 'informal assessment' from him or his assistant ombudsman. Sometimes (as with the PIA Ombudsman's office) you may receive a 'provisional assessment' from a legal officer or case officer. Both you and the organisation can usually respond to these views.

The matter may be resolved at this stage or may proceed for the ombudsman to make his **final decision**. Depending upon the ombudsman scheme, it may be termed differently, such as a determination or adjudication or formal recommendation. An ombudsman generally takes account of legal infringements such as a breach of contract. He may also note whether codes of practice have been observed.

Some ombudsmen look at **maladministration** which can cover:

- bad administration
- inefficiency
- negligence
- acting contrary to normal procedures.

Some ombudsmen can take account of **unfair treatment**. Even if something is technically lawful, it could still be unfair.

Ombudsmen do not usually have 'general' powers. It is no good, for example, asking the BS Ombudsman to order a society to pay more interest to all account-holders. His orders relate only to individuals who complain to him.

Ombudsmen will not usually interfere with commercial decisions and internal matters. Complainants who demand 'sack the manager' (or, as in one complaint, 'Shoot the directors!') are generally onto a no-hoper.

Is that it?

Usually, if you do not accept the ombudsman's decision, you can walk away with any legal rights intact and sue in court if you wish. A decision by the Pension Ombudsman is binding on you, subject to appeal to the High Court on a point of law.

Generally the organisation has virtually little option but to accept the decision provided you do. (It varies from scheme to scheme. Sometimes the alternative is to publicise reasons for not accepting, which is hardly good for public relations.)

If you accept, then the matter is usually at an end, as if you have agreed a settlement. You cannot try for more through the courts or elsewhere.

> Note that most ombudsmen cannot investigate any complaint which has been or becomes the subject of proceedings. You are unlikely to be able to take something to court, and then to an ombudsman.

Is there a trial?

No. Ombudsmen schemes are aimed at informality. Some ombudsmen occasionally hold an oral hearing, often where evidence is finely balanced and they wish to decide who they believe. It can be at their office, in a room around a table – or, if that's inconvenient (most ombudsmen being London-based) sometimes at, say, a hotel. Formalities like sworn evidence are not generally required.

Is there anyone else?

There are regulatory bodies which may be able to help perhaps when there is no ombudsman appropriate to your complaint. Examples are:

● The Registrar of Friendly Societies, who looks at complaints against Friendly Societies.

- The Complaints Bureau of the Securities and Futures Authorities, which oversees stockbrokers, futures and options dealers.

- The Investors Compensation Scheme which may help when an investment company is insolvent.

Some ombudsmen mentioned in Chapter 9 are linked to financial services, such as the Legal Services Ombudsman, the Corporate Estate Agents Ombudsman and the Inland Revenue Adjudicator.

CASE STUDIES

'Mis-sold'

Louis has an endowment mortgage which he is not sure will fully repay his mortgage at the end of the term. He suspects that a repayment mortgage/another policy would have been more suitable for him. His fears are fuelled by press reports of endowment 'mis-selling', particularly in the late eighties. He takes this up with his lender only to receive vague assertions that the endowment was 'best for his requirements.'

Louis may have grounds for complaint to an ombudsman – which one depends on several factors involved.

If the lender is a bank, the Banking Ombudsman may be appropriate, or if a building society, the BS Ombudsman. The BS Ombudsman, however, cannot consider 'pre-completion' matters (*ie* before a mortgage was implemented) prior to 1 July 1994. It may therefore depend upon when Louis received any mortgage advice, or whether he already had a mortgage with that society, and perhaps switched from repayment to endowment.

The Insurance Ombudsman has previously dealt with this type of complaint. It is more likely now that the PIA Ombudsman will be appropriate. However, there are limits on his jurisdiction relating to dates involved, and Louis will certainly have difficulty if the endowment was taken prior to 28 April 1988 (when certain Financial Services Act provisions became effective).

Louis's best bet is probably to contact the PIA Ombudsman's office to establish if they can help. If not, they should clarify which other ombudsman can.

The ghost in the machine

Anita is a busy working mother who finds cash machine facilities invaluable. She often uses the ATM near where she works to withdraw cash. One month she receives a statement showing several ATM withdrawals made in another town which she does not remember making. She queries this with her bank but is told that records show all withdrawals were made using her card and personal identification number (PIN).

On the face of it, Anita may be a victim of so-called 'phantom withdrawals'. Prior to the Code of Good Banking Practice (effective from March 1992), the Banking and BS Ombudsmen received many complaints like this. Some were shown to involve fraud but generally the customer had an uphill battle against computer records and account conditions (especially if they had teenage children living at home).

Since the introduction of the Code, a bank or building society will usually refund disputed withdrawals, with the customer's responsibility limited to £50, unless the customer acted with 'gross negligence' like keeping the card and written PIN together where they could be easily stolen or 'borrowed'.

If Anita's card was stolen, the sooner she reports this the less likely she is to bear any loss.

'Not covered'

James completes a mortgage and takes Mortgage Protection Insurance arranged through his building society. This covers twelve months' repayment if he becomes seriously ill or unemployed.

Unfortunately James later finds himself without work. He puts in a claim, but is rejected because the insurers say his line of work is classed as self-employed and is thereby excluded under the policy, and they do not pay for the first three months anyway.

James may have a case that the exclusions were not properly drawn to his attention by the building society, depending on what was said and any literature he received. Under a code of practice, the society is under an obligation to make exclusions clear.

SUMMARY

- Identify the essence of your complaint.

- Select the appropriate ombudsman.

- If you reach deadlock, contact the ombudsman's office as soon as possible.

- Submit your complaint on the appropriate form, concisely stating the facts, your grievances and your claim.

- Enclose any evidence in support of your case, including copy correspondence and witness statements where appropriate.

DISCUSSION POINTS

1. Consider which might be the best ombudsman to approach for the following claims:

   (a) that a building society investment account did not yield the 'guaranteed' interest stated in the account literature;

   (b) that your bank sold you inappropriate household insurance when you accepted its mortgage;

   (c) that you received bad advice when persuaded to take out a personal pension plan.

2. Taking the example situation given at 'Recognising your type of complaint', list the points and enclosures to include in your complaints form.

3. Suppose the example situation comes down to what was said between you and the branch manager. What sources of evidence could you use to back up your allegations?

9
Utilising Other Ombudsmen

APPROACHING THE RIGHT ONE

There is not yet an ombudsman for every complaint, but there may soon come a day when there is. There has also been a recent proposal for a general legal ombudsman.

Don't get mad, get ombudsmanned
There are still many who can help now. Figure 15 sets out some of the main adjudicators who exist (in addition to those in the financial services sector listed in Chapter 8) together with details of what they do.

Our ombudsman
Most ombudsmen here are part of the British and Irish Ombudsman Association. This sets certain standards, for example criteria for the use of the term 'ombudsman' and promotion of **best practice**.

Into Europe
An EU Ombudsman was appointed under the Maastricht Treaty, to investigate complaints against EU administrative bodies. He has received several complaints from Britons – for example, on refusal to give access to documents.

GETTING AN OMBUDSMAN'S HELP

Each ombudsman has his own procedures. Usually you do not go to them until you have passed through a lower tier of complaints administration. With the Inland Revenue Adjudicator, for example, you must first complain to your local tax office and Regional Controller.

Each office will advise you of their procedure. Many supply explanatory notes.

ADJUDICATOR FOR DIFFERENT TYPES OF COMPLAINT

Parliamentary Ombudsman

The original ombudsman introduced here in 1967. Investigates complaints referred by MPs for members of the public against alleged maladministration by government departments and agencies (such as the Data Protection Registry) leading to injustice, and complaints about the operation of the Code of Practice on Access to Government Information.

Local Commissioners

Investigate allegations of maladministration by local government and some other authorities.

Health Service Commissioners/Ombudsmen

Investigate complaints by members of the public against NHS authorities about maladministration leading to injustice or failures in providing a service, or about the Code of Practice on Openness in the NHS. It is anticipated that their powers may be extended to complaints about exercise of clinical judgement and GPs plus others providing primary care.

Legal Services Ombudsman

He oversees complaints against the legal profession. Complaints must first go through the relevant professional body, such as the **Solicitors Complaints Bureau/Office for the Supervision of Solicitors**, which look at complaints such as misconduct and over-charging. The Law Society can assist in matters of conduct.

Corporate Estate Agents Ombudsman

Investigates complaints relating to buying and selling of residential property by individuals, such as allegations of maladministration by agents, for example, inefficiency or faulty valuations for marketing purposes. Only certain companies are members of the scheme (about 20 in all, including most large chains) so some agents remain outside jurisdiction.

Housing Association Ombudsman

Investigates certain complaints covering housing associations.

Inland Revenue Adjudicator

Investigates complaints arising after 5 April 1993 relating to personal tax, for example inefficiency by the IR, but cannot question tax law as such.

Accountants Ombudsman

One was proposed by the **Institute of Chartered Accountants** to investigate complaints against its members. Complaints about investment advice and audits are taken through its **Practice Regulation Directorate**. Complaints about the professional conduct of accountants are taken through its **Professional Conduct Directorate**.

Funeral Ombudsman

Set up partly in response to concern over certain dubious selling of insurance cover for funeral expenses. Investigates some complaints about funeral directors.

Fig. 15. Other ombudsmen.

IS IT WORTH IT?

The benefits of an ombudsman's adjudication are:

- relative speed
- economy
- informality

as opposed to the court system. Often they hear matters which it would be difficult to litigate upon. They are not usually bound by strict rules of evidence and may often look further than the letter of the law, towards overall fairness.

CASE STUDIES

No sale

Alan and Linda have been trying to sell their house for some time. They feel that their estate agent has been dilatory about advertising the property. This spring, however, a couple view it and say they intend to make an offer. Alan and Linda are on tenterhooks for days, but nothing is heard from the estate agent.

Linda later bumps into the couple in the street and asks for some indication of what changed their minds. They explain that they were told by the agent that a higher offer than they had in mind had been received on Linda's property. They have since purchased another house through the same agent.

There must be grounds for complaint here, as Alan and Linda were, at the very least, not kept properly informed. It seems that another offer may have been invented, perhaps either in the hope that the potential buyers would offer more or, for some reason, so they would choose the other house. Unfortunately, a few less scrupulous agents may make it a paramount consideration to secure a chain of sales to collect several commissions on completion. It would be interesting to know if the other vendor here is buying a house from the same agent.

Alan and Linda could complain to the Corporate Estate Agents Ombudsman, if their agent is within this scheme. If so, it may help to establish what actually happened. They can also mention the lack of effort put into promoting the property.

The tax man cometh

Fraser receives a tax assessment indicating more tax to pay than he expected. He feels this is blatantly incorrect. He rings his local office to raise queries. The person dealing with the matter has clearly had a bad day, and uses some colourful language to tell Fraser that he is wrong.

In challenging the assessment, Fraser will probably have to go through the **General and Special Commissioners**. As to the rudeness he encountered, the IR Adjudicator should have jurisdiction. He will first have to complain at local level, and should contact the superior of the official he dealt with over the telephone.

Taking forever

The Stead family have suffered the bereavement of a wealthy relative. Under the will, the inheritance is to be shared amongst them. Probate is being handled by a local solicitors' firm. The length of time spent winding-up the estate is now 'winding them up'.

This is a tricky, but not uncommon complaint levelled against some solicitors. The family should seek an explanation. There may be good reason, such as inheritance tax complications. Otherwise, any redress may depend on whether any of the family is an executor and/or if a solicitor of the firm is appointed executor. The firm is primarily acting on behalf of the deceased and his executors, rather than the beneficiaries who inherit. An approach can be made to the firm which should have some form of complaints procedure. Depending upon the circumstances, the matter may be referred to the Office for The Supervision of Solicitors (OFSOL), which takes over from the Solicitors Complaints Bureau from September 1996. The Legal Services Ombudsman, who oversees complaints against solicitors, has taken a strong stance to some such matters.

SUMMARY

In any complaint, check whether a relevant ombudsman scheme might assist you. This may provide a relatively quick, inexpensive and informal process to decide the dispute.

DISCUSSION POINTS

Where might you seek redress if (a) you suspect that your accountant is lying to you or (b) your solicitor has repeated in public something which you told him in confidence.

10
Contacting Trading Standards

WHO ARE THEY?

Trading Standards Departments are local authority departments. Whilst they can certainly help you, their role is not primarily to assist in private disputes but more to preserve standards of fair trading.

The departments are manned by committed full-time Trading Standards officers. Some may be legally qualified. All have a thorough working knowledge of the laws which they enforce. They have power to take offending traders to court (usually the Magistrates' Court) if the criminal law has been broken. They may be able to obtain a compensation order for you (usually limited to £2,000 in the Magistrates' Court).

WHAT POWERS DO THEY HAVE?

Their powers relate to a number of areas, such as:

- product safety
- price markings
- counterfeit goods
- weights and measures
- trade descriptions.

They have access to specialists and laboratories who can analyse the make-up of goods and carry out stringent safety tests. Trading Standards Departments are concerned that goods are safe and **as described**.

Matters in which they become involved range from the shrinking of an Yves St Laurent suit by dry-cleaners to inadequate price lists in public houses; and from investigating the descriptions of funerals offered by undertakers to the seizing of imitation goods on market stalls. There is some overlap with the police but Trading Standards Departments concentrate mainly on **misdescription**.

Their ambit derives from many areas of legislation. Under the **Consumer Protection Act**, it is a criminal offence to give a misleading indication in the course of a business to consumers regarding price. An example is stating that goods are less than the recommended price when they are not. It is also an offence to fail to comply with a general safety standard, though some defences are available.

There are regulations to cover a wide spectrum of products such as:

- prams and pushchairs
- toy water snakes
- scented erasers
- child-resistant packaging
- babies' dummies
- fabrics
- plugs and sockets
- gas appliances
- bunk beds
- pencils
- fireworks
- cosmetics
- furniture and furnishings fire safety.

BEING MISLED BY FALSE DESCRIPTIONS

The area where Trading Standards are most likely to help in a consumer dispute relates to **trade descriptions**. The **Trade Descriptions Act 1968** applies if you purchase goods, which you find have been falsely described, such as in an advertisement or a catalogue.

Cavalier use of phrases such as 'gold' instead of 'gold-plated or 'gold effect' have sometimes caught retailers out (not to mention 'Guinness is good for you'). An altered odometer reading relating to a car's mileage can amount to a false trade description.

Other matters which form part of a trade description and must be correct are:

- quantity or size, *eg* size 10
- method of manufacture *eg* hand-made
- composition *eg* 100 per cent recycled
- fitness for purpose/performance *eg* child-proof
- testings undertaken/result *eg* full MOT
- approvals which apply *eg* British Standards
- place/date of manufacture *eg* made in Great Britain (This is

something which is currently under scrutiny at European level.)

The Trade Descriptions Act can also help if you find false statements were made about facilities, accommodation or services. This can be relevant to package holidays (see also Chapter 2).

Caught in the act

To be 'false' a trade description has to be false to a **material degree**, not just a very minor discrepancy. A seller has a defence if the false statement arose from a cause beyond his control and he has been diligent and taken reasonable precautions. Therefore if he relied on false information from a supplier, which he did his best to verify, he might not be guilty.

However if he is guilty, the matter may also be reported to the **Office of Fair Trading**. The Director-General there can start procedures to stop practices which are harmful to consumers and/or to take action against traders who persist in unfair trading.

APPROACHING TRADING STANDARDS

If you have a complaint which overlaps with one of the fields dealt with by Trading Standards, you should contact your local department. The number will be in the telephone directory, usually as a sub-category under the name of your local authority.

Involving Trading Standards can be a powerful incentive to a trader to resolve your grievance – sometimes even more so than involving your solicitor and/or suing in the County Court. Trading Standards can bring a prosecution in the criminal courts, which carries more stigma. Furthermore the press may pick up on it, which can be damaging to business.

CASE STUDIES

'It's a bargain'

Varun purchases a telephone answering machine which the shop has marked as 'Bargain! Reduced to £30'. Once back home, he sets it up. He is amazed to find that a pre-recorded message is already installed in it, informing callers that 'Jilly regrets she is not able to take their call but hopes that they will leave a message after the tone'. Furthermore, the machine has poor sound quality, and is as much a bargain as Monty Python's infamous piston engine.

Varun takes the machine back to the shop, where an assistant points to a notice on the wall stating, 'No refunds on sale goods'. Furious he walks out.

Varun could follow the procedure of raising a complaint as described in Chapter 3. Clearly his statutory rights, such as the condition for satisfactory quality, have been infringed. In these circumstances, however, contacting Trading Standards quickly is a wise course. Several offences may have been committed – from the vague statement about a reduction placed upon the goods to the invalid exclusion notice displayed in the shop (see Chapter 2). Furthermore, it seems that used goods are being sold as if new.

Trading Standards may investigate and prosecute. If the retailer can show a one-off mistake and that procedures are implemented to prevent reoccurrence, they may be lenient this time. Varun should, however, receive full compensation from the shop which may well be topped-up with an amount for goodwill.

'It's a good little bus'

Les telephones a number given in a newspaper advertisement concerning a low-mileage car for sale. He arranges to meet the seller at a given address, which is in a residential area. The seller and car are waiting for him in the street. Les test-drives the car, which handles well. The mileometer reads 11,000 miles. The seller produces the registration documents and explains that the address is different due to a recent move. He gives verbal assurances that the car is in good condition. Les concludes the purchase.

Within a few weeks, Les experiences problems with the car. He has it checked in a garage and several faults are discovered and doubt is cast on the mileage. Les goes back to where he met the seller, to be told by residents that he is not at that address.

It seems that Les has been fleeced. The seller may be a car dealer, posing as a private seller to bolster confidence and because a private sale gives fewer statutory rights (see Chapter 2). With hindsight, Les should have taken more care, perhaps paying a mechanic or the AA or RAC to check the car before he purchased it. The verbal assurance given by the seller is similar to one which was held to be misrepresentation in a legal case where a dealer made it. Unfortunately it will be difficult to prove, even if he can trace the seller. At the very least, taking a friend along as a witness to what was said, would have been a good idea.

As regards the mileage, Les should have looked for tell-tale signs of 'clocking', such as worn pedal rubbers, and checked past MOT certificates. He should now contact Trading Standards. They make a valiant effort against this type of offence, even in the face of new technology making it easier to perpetrate. They will be very interested in the activities of any dealer pretending to be a private seller.

Getting the boot

Nicola is a teenager who finds it difficult to stretch her pocket money to buy all the clothes she would like. One Sunday she attends a car boot sale and buys a pair of Levi jeans from a man, who assures her that they are genuine. The price is reasonable and she is well pleased until a few days later, when the seams fray.

Nicola seeks the advice of Trading Standards. They confirm that the jeans are not genuine Levis because certain stitching, particularly around the label, betrays this. They feel that it is likely that she bought from a trader, so in theory she has full statutory rights (see Chapter 2). The problem will be showing that he is a trader – and locating him. She could try the car boot sale site the next weekend, but he is likely to have moved on. Trading Standards Officers may also attend to investigate any further sale of counterfeit goods. Even if the trader is present, police back-up is not always immediately available and the officers have to rely on making a citizen's arrest – not to mention their own physical agility, as dodgy traders usually make a quick getaway.

SUMMARY

- In any complaint, be alert to aspects upon which you can involve your local Trading Standards Department.

- Bear in mind that a compensation order can sometimes be obtained, following a conviction in any prosecution.

- In the Magistrates' Court, such compensation is usually limited to £2,000 for each offence convicted.

- Trading Standards (or you, yourself) can report a relevant matter to the Office of Fair Trading. The Director-General there tries to stop harmful practices and unfair trading.

DISCUSSION POINTS

1. You purchase 'banana flavoured' ice cream. Consider whether the flavour should necessarily come from bananas. What if it was described as 'banana flavour'?

2. You buy a dress in the sale marked 'button missing'. At home, you find a tear in the seam. What redress might you have, if any?

3. List the documents and other matters you should check when buying a second-hand car. What kind of discrepancies could you report to Trading Standards?

Glossary

The general meaning of terms used in this book are given below. (Words can have a more particular definition in some contexts, such as for the purposes of certain legislation.)

Advocate. Someone who presents a case.

Affidavit. A statement in writing made upon oath sworn before a person, such as a solicitor, who is authorised to administer oaths.

Alternative Dispute Resolution. An alternative to court proceedings, often involving mediation.

Arbitration. The determination of a dispute other than by a full formal trial in court.

Barristers. Qualified professionals who assist clients introduced through solicitors in legal problems and proceedings.

Case law. Body of legal precedents, comprising decisions in previous law cases.

Circuit Judge. A full-time judge who often sits in the County Court or Crown Court.

Citizens Advice Bureaux. Local centres providing general advice to the public.

Civil law. In context of the law of England and Wales, the law (such as relating to contract and tort) which applies to individuals and which is enforceable through the civil courts, like the County Court and High Court.

Consideration. In broad terms as it applies to contract law, a promise or similar incentive given by one party to persuade another party to enter a contract.

Consumer. An individual acting outside any business. (The guidelines given in this book are primarily aimed at consumers.)

Contempt of court. An action in defiance of a court, sometimes for example through being rude to a presiding judge or disobeying a court order.

Contract. A legally binding agreement.

Contributory negligence. Arises where someone suffers through another's negligence, but is partly to blame for this himself.

Costs. Legal fees and expenses.

Counsel. Another word used for a barrister.

County Courts. The courts which hear most civil disputes.

Damages. Money compensation awarded by the courts.

Data Protection Act. Regulations over the holding of information about people on computer. May soon extend to manually shared information.

Defendant. Person against whom a civil action is brought.

District Judge. A judge who deals with more minor trials and some other matters in the County Court.

Evidence. Something used to prove or disprove a matter which is in issue.

General damages. In broad terms, damages awarded to compensate for general suffering as opposed to specific financial loss.

Hearsay evidence. In general, evidence which is based on something reported to a witness by someone else, rather than something which the witness has actually observed or experienced himself.

High Court. The court in which some major civil disputes are heard.

Injunction. A court order to prevent, or sometimes compel, certain action.

Internal Complaints Procedure. The process adopted by an organisation to handle complaints.

Jurisdiction. Boundaries of power held by a person or body.

Law. References in this book are **generally to the law of England and Wales** and as it applies mainly to British persons.

Legal aid. Government financial assistance given to those who qualify for help in legal matters, mainly involving court proceedings.

Legal executive. A person who has certain legal qualifications specified by the Institute of Legal Executives.

Legislation. Laws embodied in forms such as Acts of Parliament or statutory instruments.

Letter before action. Usually the final letter threatening court proceedings before they are instigated.

Liability. Fault or responsibility in law.

Liquidated damages. In broad terms, damages for a specific amount, such as, in the County Court, cost of repairs to a car damaged in a road accident caused by negligence.

Litigant in person. Someone acting for themselves rather than being represented by a solicitor.

Litigation. In general, the process of bringing a case to court.

Magistrates. Mainly non-legally qualified persons who act as judges in certain criminal cases. Also known as justices of the peace.

Maladministration. This can cover negligence, incompetence, delay and general inefficiency. (Also defined in the 'Crossman Catalogue' in relation to government.)

Ombudsman. Someone appointed to judge in certain disputes.

Plaintiff. Person bringing a civil court action.

Pleadings. Documents used in litigation by which parties in a court case set out their respective cases.

Privity of contract. A legally recognised relationship between parties, and the legal doctrine which basically states that only parties to a contract are those who can enforce or derive rights under it (though there are exceptions).

Prosecute. To pursue criminal proceedings.

Puisne judge. A type of judge mainly in the High Court.

Recorder. A part-time circuit judge.

Registrar. The old name used for a type of district judge.

Seller or supplier. A person/partnership/company who sells or supplies goods or services for purposes relating to business.

Settlement. Agreement reached to resolve a dispute without a judge's decision.

Small claims court. Section of the County Court dealing mostly with claims up to £3,000.

Solicitors. Qualified professionals who assist clients in general legal matters.

Special Damages. In broad terms, damages to compensate for a specific financial loss.

Statute. Legislation/Act of Parliament.

Strict liability. Liability without necessarily being to blame.

Sue. To pursue civil proceedings.

Tort. A civil wrong (not arising from a contract) for which an individual can sue in the civil courts.

Trading Standards Departments. Local authority departments set up to check certain legal requirements are observed by traders.

Useful Addresses

Accident Line, The Law Society, Freepost, London WC2A 1BR. Tel: (0500) 192939.

Adjudicator for National Savings, Room 106, Treasury Chambers, Parliament Street, London SW1P 3AG.

Advertising Standards Authority, 2 Torrington Place, London WC1E 7HW. Tel: (0171) 580 4100.

Arbitration Service of the Chartered Institute of Arbitrators, 24 Angel Gate, City Road, London EC1V 2RS. Tel: (0171) 837 4483.

Association for Consumer Research, 2 Marylebone Road, London NW1 4DX.

Association of British Travel Agents, 55–57 Newman Street, London W1P 4AH. Tel: (0171) 637 2444.

Association of Independent Tour Operators, 133a St Margaret's Road, Twickenham, Middlesex TW1 1RG. Tel: (0181) 744 9280.

Banking Ombudsman, 70 Grays Inn Road, London WC1X 8NB. Tel: (0171) 404 9944.

British Association of Lawyer Mediators, The Shooting Lodge, Guildford Road, Sutton Green, Guildford GU4 7PZ. Tel: (01483) 235000.

British Association of Removers, 3 Churchill Court, 58 Station Road, North Harrow, Middlesex HA2 7SA. Tel: (0181) 861 3331.

British Carpet Technical Centre, Wira House, West Park Ring Road, Leeds LS16 6QL. Tel: (0113) 2591999.

British Standards Institution, 389 Chiswick High Road, Chiswick, London W4 4AL. Tel: (0181) 996 9000.

British Tourist Authority, Blacks Road, London W6 9EL. Tel: (0181) 741 2443.

Broadcasting Complaints Commission, 5–8 The Sanctuary, London SW1P 3JS. Tel: (0171) 233 0544.

Building Societies Association, 3 Savile Row, London W1X 1AF. Tel: (0171) 437 0655.

Building Societies Ombudsman, Millbank Tower, Millbank, London SW1P 4XS. Tel: (0171) 931 0044.

Commissioner for Local Administration in England, 21 Queen Anne's Gate, London SW1H 9BU. Tel: (0171) 915 3210.

Commissioner for Local Administration in Wales, Court Road, Bridgend, Mid Glamorgan CF31 1BN. Tel: (01656) 661235.

Companies Registration Office, Companies House, Maindy, Cardiff CF4 3UZ. Tel: (01222) 388588

Confederation for the Registration of Gas Installers, St Martin's House, 140 Tottenham Court Road, London W1P 9LN.

Confederation of British Industry, Centre Point, New Oxford Street, London WC1S 1DU.

Consumers' Association Ltd, 2 Marylebone Road, London NW1 4DF. Tel: (0171) 830 6000.

Corporate Estate Agents Ombudsman, Beckitt House, 4 Bridge Street, Salisbury SP1 2LX. Tel: (01722) 333306.

Council for Licensed Conveyancers, 16 Glebe Road, Chelmsford, Essex CM1 1QG. Tel: (01245) 349599.

Data Protection Registrar, Wycliffe House, Water Lane, Wilmslow, Cheshire SK9 5AF. Tel: (01625) 545745.

Federation of Master Builders, 14–15 Great James Street, London WC1N 3DP. Tel: (0171) 242 7583.

FIMBRA, (now part of P.I.A.) Hertsmere House, Marsh Wall, London E14 9RW. Tel: (0171) 538 8860.

Funeral Ombudsman, Suite 3.3, 31 Southampton Row, London WC1B 5HJ. Tel: (0171) 430 1112.

Gas Consumers Council, Abford House, 15 Wilton Road, London SW1V 1LT. Tel: (0171) 931 9151.

General Council of the Bar, 3 Bedford Row, London WC1R 4DB. Tel: (0171) 242 0082.

General Medical Council, 178 Great Portland Street, London W1N 6JE. Tel: (0171) 580 7642.

Glass and Glazing Federation, 44–48 Borough High Street, London SE1 1XB. Tel: (0171) 403 7177.

Hairdressing Council, 12 David House, 45 High Street, South Norwood, London SE25 6HJ. Tel: (0181) 771 6205.

Health Commissioner for Scotland, Ground Floor, 1 Atholl Place, Edinburgh EH3 8HP. Tel: (0131) 225 7465.

Health Commissioner for Wales, Fourth Floor, Pearl Assurance House, Greyfriars Road, Cardiff CF1 3AG. Tel: (01222) 394621.

Health Service Ombudsman, 13th Floor, Millbank Tower, Millbank, London SW1P 4QP. Tel: (0171) 276 2035.

Heating and Ventilating Contractors Association, 34 Palace Court, London W2 4JG.

Hire Purchase Information plc, PO Box 61, Dolphin House, New Street, Salisbury, Wiltshire SP1 2TB. Tel: (01722) 422422.

Housing Association Ombudsman, Palladium House, 1–4 Argyll Street, London W1V 1AD. Tel: (0171) 437 1422.

IMRO, Lloyds Chambers, 1 Portsoken Street, London E1 8BT. Tel: (0171) 390 5000.

Inland Revenue Adjudicator, Third Floor, Haymarket House, 28 Haymarket, London SW1Y 4SP. Tel: (0171) 930 2292.

Institute of Automotive Engineer Assessors, Mansell House, 22 Bore Street, Lichfield, Staffordshire WS13 6LP. Tel: (01543) 251346.

Institute of Chartered Accountants of England and Wales, Practice Regulation

Directorate, Chartered Accountants Hall, PO Box 433, Moorgate Place, London EC2P 2BJ. Tel: (0171) 920 8100.

Professional Conduct Directorate, Gloucester House, Silbury Boulevard, Central Milton Keynes MK9 2HL. Tel: (01908) 248100.

Institute of Plumbing, 64 Station Lane, Hornchurch, Essex RM12 6NB. Tel: (01708) 472791.

Institute of Trading Standards, 3–5 Hadleigh Business Centre, 351 London Road, Hadleigh, Essex SS7 2BT. Tel: (01702) 559922.

Insurance Brokers Registration Council. 67, St Mary's Axe, London EC3A 8NB. Tel: (0171) 621 1061.

Insurance Ombudsman, City Gate One, 135 Park Street, London SE1 9EA. Tel: (0171) 928 7600.

International Consumer Policy Bureau, 32/8 Castle Terrace, Edinburgh EH1 2EL. Tel: (0131) 228 3732.

Investment Ombudsman, 6 Frederick's Place, London EC2R 8BT. Tel: (0171) 796 3065.

Investors Compensation Scheme, Gaverelle House, 2-14 Bunhill Row, London EC1Y 8RA. Tel: (0171) 628 8820.

Land Charges Department, Barrington Way, Plymouth PL5 3LP.

LAUTRO, (now part of P.I.A.) 1 Canada Square, Canary Wharf, London E14 5AZ. Tel: (0171) 538 8860.

Law Society of England & Wales, Law Society House, 113 Chancery Lane, London WC2A 1PL. Tel: (0171) 242 1222.

Legal Aid Board, 85 Gray's Inn Road, London WC1X 8AA. Tel: (0171) 813 1000.

Legal Services Ombudsman, 22 Oxford Court, Oxford Street, Manchester M2 3WQ. Tel: (0161) 236 9532.

Mail Order Protection Scheme (MOPS), 16 Tooks Court, London EC4A 1LB. Tel: (0171) 405 6806.

Mail Order Traders' Association, 100 Old Hall Street, Liverpool L3 9TD. Tel: (0151) 227 4181.

Mediation UK, 82A Gloucester Road, Bishopstone, Bristol BS7 8BN. Tel: (0117) 924 1234.

Motor Agents Association Ltd, National Conciliation Service, 73 Park Street, Bristol BS1 5PS.

National Association of Citizens' Advice Bureaux, 115-123 Pentonville Road, London N1 9LZ. Tel: (0171) 833 2181.

National Association of Plumbing, Heating & Mechanical Services Contractors, 14–15 Ensign House, Ensign Business Centre, Westwood Way, Coventry, West Midlands CV4 8JA.

National Consumer Council, 20 Grosvenor Gardens, London SW1W ODH. Tel: (0171) 730 3469.

National Federation of Consumer Groups, 12 Moseley Street, Newcastle upon Tyne NE1 1DE.

National Federation of Roofing Contractors, 24 Weymouth Street, London W1N 4LX. Tel: (0171) 436 0387.

National Register of Warranted Builders, 14–15 Great James Street, London

WC1N 3DP.

Occupational Pensions Advisory Service, 11 Belgrave Road, London SW1V 1RB. Tel: (0171) 233 8080.

OFFER, 11 Belgrave Road, London SW1V 1RB. Tel: (0171) 233 6366.

Office for the Supervision of Solicitors, Victoria Court, 8 Dormer Place, Leamington Spa CV32 5AE. Tel: (01926) 820082.

Office of Fair Trading, Field House, 15–25 Bream's Buildings, London EC4A 1PR. Tel: (0171) 242 2858.

OFGAS, 130 Wilton Road, London SW1V 1LQ. Tel: (0171) 828 0898.

OFTEL, 50 Ludgate Hill, London EC4M 7JJ. Tel: (0171) 6348 700.

OFWAT, 15–17 Ridgemount Street, London WC1E 7AH. Tel: (0171) (0345) 581 658.

Oyez Publishing, Oyez House, PO Box 55, 7 Spa Road, London SE16 3QQ. Tel: (0171) 232 1000.

Parliamentary Ombudsman, Office of the Parliamentary Commissioner for Administration, Church House, Great Smith Street, London SW1P 3BW.

Pensions Ombudsman, 11 Belgrave Road, London SW1V 1RB. Tel: (0171) 834 9144.

Personal Investment Authority, 1 Canada Square, Canary Wharf, London E14 5AZ. Tel: (0171) 538 8860.

Personal Investment Authority Ombudsman, Centre Point, 103 Oxford Street, London WC1A 1QH. Tel: (0171) 240 3838. (NB Soon to move to Hartsmere House, Hartsmere Row, London E14 4AB. Tel: (0171) 538 8860).

Registrar of Friendly Societies, 16 Great Riglborough Road, London W1V 2AX. Tel: (0171) 437 0992.

Retail Motor Industry Federation, 201 Great Portland Street, London W1N 6AB. Tel: (0171) 580 9122.

Royal Institute of Chartered Surveyors, 12 Great George Street, London SW1P 3AD. Tel: (0171) 222 7000.

Securities and Futures Authority Complaints Bureau, Cottons Centre, Cottons Lane, London SE1 2QB. Tel: (0171) 378 9000.

Securities and Investment Board, Gaverelle House, 2–14 Bunhill Row, London EC1Y 8RA. Tel: (0171) 638 1240.

Society of Master Shoe Repairers Ltd, St Crispin's House, 21 Station Road, Desborough, Northants NN14 2SA. Tel: (01536) 760374.

Society of Motor Manufacturers and Traders Ltd, Forbes House, Halkin Street, London SW1X 7DS.

Solicitors Complaints Bureau, Victoria Court, 8 Dormer Place, Leamington Spa CV32 5AE. Tel: (01926) 820082.

Solicitors Indemnity Fund, 100 St Johns Street, London EC1M 4EH. Tel: (0171) 566 6000.

Textile Services Association Ltd, 7 Churchill Court, 58 Station Road, North Harrow, Middlesex HA2 7SA. Tel: (0181) 863 7755/9177.

Vehicle Builders and Repairers Association Conciliation Service, Belmont House, Gildersome, Leeds LS27 7TW.

Further Reading

Applying to an Industrial Tribual, Trevor Naylor (How To Books, 1992).

Ask for the Moon and Get It, Percy Ross with Dick Sanson (Thorsons, 1989).

The Business of Assertiveness, Rennie Fritchie and Maggie Melling (BBC Books, 1991).

Consumer Law, Peter M Walker (Pearson Professional Publishing Limited, 1995, 3rd edn.).

The Law of Consumer Protection and Fair Trading, (Butterworths, 1992, 4th edn.).

The Litigation Handbook, Alan Matthews (Fitzwarren Publishing, 1995).

Managing Your Personal Finances, John Claxton (How To Books, 1996).

Practical Legal Aid, Ian Pollard (Longman).

Sale of Goods Litigation, F Philpott and R Spearman (Longman).

The Small Claims Court, George Appleby (Tolley).

Tactics, Edward de Bono (Harper Collins, 1993).

Index